Perfect
Love

Bill —
Blessings for your
Perfect Love!

Jan A Burch

Perfect Love

*How to Find Yours
and Make It Last Forever*

BRAD AND JAN LUNDY

Heart to Heart Press
Traverse City, MI

Heart to Heart Press
P.O. Box 427
Traverse City, MI 49685

Cover & interior design: Jan Lundy and Michael Dudek
Editing: Claire Gerus
Typography: Michael Dudek
Cover photo: Mira
Interior photos: iStockphoto

Library of Congress Control Number: 2006920247

First Printing, March 2006
ISBN 0-9663602-8-1
ISBN 978-0-9663602-8-8

♲ Printed in Canada by Friesens Corporation on 100% postconsumer waste recycled paper

To J.C.

for
inspiration

To Mother Earth

for
life and love

CONTENTS

Part II The Perfect Love Toolbox

Part III   The Shores of Perfect Love

*Out beyond ideas of wrongdoing and rightdoing,
there is a field.*

I'll meet you there.

Jelaluddin Rumi

INTRODUCTION

Imagine what it would feel like each morning to wake up in gratitude for the person lying next to you, turn and warmly welcome one another, to hold each other in loving arms, where you rest in blissful silence or talk quietly of matters of the heart. No matter what is shared, you both know you will be deeply listened to and unconditionally loved.

Imagine being so connected with your partner throughout the day that you can't wait to be reunited. You bask in your partner's smile and feel his or her loving presence. To be physically close, to talk and share the events of your day, the joys and the challenges. Supreme confidants, divine friends always.

Imagine that when your day draws to a close and evening comes, you lie down together once more, eager to connect in an even deeper way. To touch one another so that all notion of separation disappears. To surrender all differences, all boundaries, all physicality, so there is only peace. There is only one being present, one essence. Love is your name. Oneness is who you are together.

Sound unrealistic, implausible? Reserved for a select few enlightened or lucky souls? Hardly. *Anyone* can experience Perfect Love like this if they truly desire it. Despite what you may have been told, Perfect Love can be yours. It is simply a matter of choice, as you will see...

7

The Voyage Begins...

BRAD: *It's the early 1980s and I've just purchased a book whose cover grips me—a photograph of a couple tenderly kissing—and I'm overtaken by an intense desire to be in a partnership like they are. I'd gone through a devastating divorce a few years earlier and was feeling quite alone. How I yearned for a real partner. I kept looking at the image, fantasizing what a relationship like this might feel like. It occupied my thoughts daily.*

A knowing began to grow in me that I could actually have it, a relationship like nothing I'd ever had before, though I wasn't sure how to go about it. I was not fond of the idea of being in a traditional relationship again. It was too much work, too much negotiating and bargaining, too much arguing. I found myself thinking, "If I'm going to have another relationship, I've got to build it my way. I've got to do it differently." I didn't know what that meant or even how to begin, but I trusted I would be shown the way.

JAN: *I too had a deep longing for true love. Like many women of my generation, I believed in the fairy-tale relationship. My prince would come, sweep me off my feet, and we'd ride off into the sunset pledging undying love for one another. In my mid to late twenties, I suddenly realized the fairy tale was a myth and an intimate relationship was hard work, or so it seemed. Little romance, not much fun. I kept hoping for more, though, certain that if I just kept trying, read one more relationship book, went to one more marriage counseling session, I could make my relationship better.*

My longing to experience profound and lasting love grew. But no matter how hard I tried, I couldn't seem to create it in my life. It felt too difficult, unattainable. Finally, I gave up altogether. I shifted my focus inward, toward healing myself and my relationship wounds, in time even surrendering my need to be in a relationship. I partnered myself and moved into greater happiness. I no longer felt that longing to know true love, but I must still have been open to receiving it or I wouldn't have recognized it when it came knocking on my door when it did.

It seems Spirit did indeed have a special kind of Love in mind for both of us. In the fall of 2000 we came together to discuss a business venture (he a publisher, she a writer), and within twenty minutes of our meeting, we both knew our connection was not about business at all but something much more powerful. The intensity of our feelings took us by surprise, as neither of us was actively looking for a love relationship, just a productive business partnership.

Yet, there was a remembering of who we might be to one another—a soul recognition, if you will. Intuitively, somehow, we knew that we would be companioning each other from that moment on. We shared our hesitancy about being in an intimate partnership again and agreed that the "old way" wasn't good enough for us. If we were going to enter into a loving partnership, it had to be very different than anything we'd experienced before. We committed ourselves to finding a "new way" of being together. What we discovered was "Perfect Love."

For over five years now, we have been living this new model of relationship, one co-created with guidance from Spirit. More often, however, it seemed we learned how to live this model the hard way—two steps forward and one step back. We had hundreds of arguments and many disillusioning moments. Jokingly, we reminded each other of Dick and Liz in the film version of *Who's Afraid of Virginia Woolf,* the pain and drama of our relationship overshadowing any possible joy. Today we know it was truly a miracle that we not only stayed together, but thrived, moving into the deepest experience of Love we have ever known. Despite the hardships, we felt Spirit's presence through it all, urging us on, revealing insights and techniques to keep our connection strong, our spirits joined. Our angelic helpers were constantly there to lend support. A passionate desire to eventually arrive at a place of effortless relationship and share it with others kept us moving forward instead of giving up.

Thankfully, your journey to Perfect Love does not have to be as "boulder strewn" as ours. Though, sometimes, when people hear our story, they doubt that Love like ours could exist for them. We're here to tell you that nothing could be further from the truth. What you are holding in your hands is the road map we have created to help you realize Perfect Love, just as we have, only with fewer bumps in the road. We've done much of the groundwork for you, so your path will be easier to walk.

Perfect Love is real and available to you right now. You will discover through this body of work that Perfect Love is not something to be achieved. It is truly a state of mind, heart, and soul—a state of being. It is as simple and as complex as an adjustment in perception, a shift in consciousness. And in that, it is simply profound.

You see, Perfect Love is who we really are in our essence. It is our true nature. We are Perfect Love because we come from a divine source—Spirit—which is Love. And because we are Spirit at our core, we, too, are the embodiment of Love—naturally. We have not been told this, however, nor have we been taught how to live practically, as such, in our human, day-to-day world.

This book presents a method we've discovered to help you tap into your personal experience of Perfect Love. We call it "Soul Sailing™." Soul Sailing is a series of techniques that can show you how to be in relationship with another as the spiritual being you are—as your "Spirit self." Applying Soul Sailing to your everyday life will enable you to put an end to frustrating, ego-dominated relationships. Only then can you experience Perfect Love beyond your wildest dreams with an intimate partner and, in time, with every person you meet.

In Part I, "Setting the Course for Love," you will be reintroduced to your Spirit self and also to your "Ego Operating System," the mental/emotional system within you that is dominated by the ego. You will learn how to recognize when you are operating as your Spirit self or as your ego self, and understand how to move from one to the other through the power of "Vibration." By consciously choosing thoughts, words, and actions that contain the Vibration of Love, you will begin to experience more and more Love, inner peace, and joy in every aspect of your daily life. You will also be shown why it is so exciting to do this work within an intimate relationship and how to begin that process with your partner.

In Part II, you will find the " The Perfect Love Toolbox," tried and true methods that enable you and your partner to connect more deeply to one another and to your Spirit selves, developing a solid foundation where Love can flourish. We call these "Love Links." When difficulties arise (as they inevitably will), "Ego

Busters" are techniques to help you weather relationship storms together. And, if the going gets a bit tough and you find yourself disconnected from one another's spirit, "Heart Menders" will bring you back together.

Part III, "The Shores of Perfect Love," will inspire you to see what life can be like if you apply Soul Sailing principles to all your relationships. You'll begin to see the bigger picture of how Perfect Love can transform the world as we know it. You'll also find assistance for your personal journey through the Perfect Love Support Network, and answers to your most frequently asked questions. By joining our hearts and energies in this way, we can put this transformational material to good use and usher in a future of grand possibility for us all.

Who Should Read *Perfect Love*?

As we began to tell others about this book, we often heard the same response: "Do you have to be in a relationship to read it?" The fact of the matter is, Soul Sailing is for everybody, whether you are in an intimate partnership or not. It is a way of living, a way of being in relationship with every person who comes into your life. By applying Soul Sailing principles (and using the techniques in the Perfect Love Toolbox), you have the opportunity to deepen and authenticate every relationship in your life—from the most casual to the most intimate.

You see, this journey to Perfect Love is really an individual journey. As you will read, being in relationship with another is really about being in relationship with yourself. To have a Spirit-filled relationship with another person, you must first do the work of self. By this we mean connecting with your Spirit self and operating from that space as much as possible. It is your unique opportunity to diminish the ego's hold on you so that you can bring your whole, grand self to any relationship in the future.

If you are single, this book is for you. Rest assured that if you begin to apply what you learn here, forthcoming relationships will be dramatically different than any you've ever had before. You can practice on friends and colleagues, use the tools in the Perfect Love Toolbox and see the magic of this material at work right now, so when your intimate partner does arrive, you will be ready.

If you are in an intimate partnership, this book is for you. Some of you will have partners who will eagerly jump into this material with you because you're both ready to experience profound Love. Some of you will have a reluctant or even uninvolved partner, and that is alright, too. Remember, Soul Sailing is about doing the work of self to give you a greater experience of what it is like to live as Spirit. Whether your partner participates or not, you will grow and change. You will become more radiant and love-filled.

Whether you are in an intimate relationship or not, be forewarned that when you begin to operate as your Spirit self, you will become absolutely magnetic. People will want to spend time with you, and be close to you. They'll wish to be in relationship with you because you are perfectly irresistible—a reflection of Perfect Love. Therefore, we have written this book in language that assumes you are or will be in an intimate partnership.

Your world as you know it is *about to change*. The voyage you are embarking on is the journey of a lifetime, and we are here to support you every step of the way. We'll remain your companions for as long as you like, for that's what this life journey is truly all about—caring, sharing, and being present for one another. Everybody can have an experience of Perfect Love. Yours awaits!

HOW TO USE THIS BOOK

A Few Words of Advice to Soul Sailing Travelers

Perfect Love presents concepts and terms you may have never heard of before. That's because it is calling you to a completely new way of thinking and operating in the world. In fact, at times, it may even feel as if we are speaking a foreign language, expecting you to learn by osmosis how to converse, live, and Love within a whole new framework. We are! But we also know that such a monumental shift in perception doesn't happen overnight. As you will hear us say throughout this text, mastering the principles we present here takes time, plenty of patience, and practice. Therefore, we offer this sage advice:

> ## ☙ Have compassion for yourself.

Because you are embarking on a transformational journey, don't be surprised if you bump up against some resistance. It may come from others who are skeptical that such a thing as Perfect Love is possible. Or it might come from your own Ego Operating System as it puts you on a roller-coaster ride of wild emotions, including self-doubt and fear. Any major life change amplifies the ego self because the ego may feel as if it is losing control, and it is! That's exactly what happens when Perfect Love comes to call. Your ego self is being asked to take a backseat to your Spirit self and it may not like it one single bit.

So, show yourself and your partner some compassion. Know that it is absolutely normal for your egos to act up and act out as you continue to embrace yourselves and each other as Spirit. Love one another, no matter what your egos say or do. Be the Love you wish to receive and, in time, you'll feel a shift. There will be fewer bumps in the road as the ego and its influence begins to fall away. Peace will begin to replace anger and anxiety. Your relationships will flourish and life will get easier.

⁊ Practice, Practice, Practice

Read *Perfect Love* as many times as you can to truly familiarize yourself with its content and the tools in the Toolbox. The more readings the better!

Take time to reflect upon the questions or exercises suggested at the end of each chapter. This will enable you to integrate the material into your thought processes and seek out ways to put the principles into action with the people you love. We also recommend keeping a Soul Sailing journal. When you commit yourself to actual reflection time, especially writing down the awarenesses that come, you can see where you may be stuck, shedding light on ego-debilitating patterns of operating. You can also witness your growth and movement toward Spirit.

Make a pact with a special friend to do Soul Sailing together and be study buddies. You can be a great support system to one another as you practice the techniques presented here.

Visit www.soulsailing.com to learn how to form a study group with friends and get together to talk about what you read. The Website can provide additional support for your group, along with topics of discussion. Connect with other Soul Sailing travelers and share your experiences at the Community Forum on the Website.

Make good use of the Perfect Love Toolbox Quick Reference Guide on page 128 when you need a speedy reminder of Soul Sailing techniques. Make copies of it and carry it with you. Refer to it often.

ॐ Ask for Help

"I get by with a little help from my friends," is the refrain from an old Beatles' tune and it certainly applies to this journey to Perfect Love. That is why we've created www.soulsailing.com, to give you the support and companionship you'll need when you're just getting started. On page 155, you can learn more about the Perfect Love Network, the best way to stay connected to this material and to your Spirit self. It's enlightening, entertaining, and informative. We look forward to meeting you there!

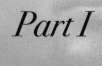

Part I

*Setting the Course
for Love*

Divinity is my true nature. I am a soul among souls.

JULIA CAMERON

*When you perceive yourself as spirit,
you will not simply feel love—you will be love.*

DEEPAK CHOPRA

CHAPTER 1

CHARTING YOUR COURSE

There is one thing we all have in common. Each of us wants to be loved. From the moment of our birth, we instinctively reach out to touch others, to feel their warmth, to be intimately connected with them. No matter our age or path in life, the desire to experience love never ends.

At certain times in our lives, we may even find ourselves longing for it, consumed by the need to feel its comforting embrace or to be immersed in its fiery passion. Others spin fantasies about finding the perfect partner with whom they'll spend a lifetime of romance and undying devotion. If we are honest, none of us can imagine living without love from a very special someone.

So, we search for love, setting out on a quest at an early age to find "the one." Some of us literally hunt for them; others sit and wait for them to show up. We're confident that our soul mate exists. That's what we've been told for a very long time now. There is someone tailor-made just for you. Somewhere, your perfect partner awaits.

We're here to tell you to stop looking and stop waiting. There are no perfect partners. There is only Perfect Love.

Perfect Love is available to you right here, right now. It's as close to you as your breath. It's inside of you, all around you, and, most importantly, immediately accessible. You just haven't tapped into it—until now.

To uncover the Perfect Love that awaits you is a simple process, one which begins with a shift in perception. If you are ready to let go of everything you have ever been told about love, your world as you know it is going to dramatically change, and you'll set sail on the journey of a lifetime—the journey to experience the greatest love you have ever known.

To Love Perfectly

For thousands of years now, the ancient wise ones—masters, saints, and yogis of all religions and spiritual persuasions—have known how to access Perfect Love, but rarely was it within reach of the average person. Their approach might take years, even lifetimes, of study, practice, and personal sacrifice. Today, we are able to offer you a new, more direct way to access the highest form of Love. We have come to call this method "Soul Sailing." It is a natural, organic approach to uncovering the Perfect Love that we can all experience each and every day. Using this method, Perfect Love is available to every man, woman, and child who desires to welcome it into their lives.

We base our Soul Sailing approach on one basic truth:

We are Spirit beings having a human experience. *

---

* *"Spirit" is the word we have chosen throughout this writing to represent God, the All, the Infinite Source of which we are a part.*

If you are a seeker, you may have heard this concept before, even attempted to live this truth on your own. The problem is, no one has ever really taught us how to live in this very physical (and human) universe as spiritual beings. True, we may believe that we are divinely sourced and connected. We strive to embody spiritual principles and incorporate spiritual practices into our daily lives. Yet, despite all our good intentions at "being spiritual," we remain human beings through and through, trying our best to live a more spiritual existence.

The result of these attempts to "be spiritual" can be frustrating to us. We have momentary experiences of spiritual qualities—inner peace, abundance or joy, for example—but these moments do not seem to last. We feel them for a short time, minutes or hours, and then suddenly they are gone, and other less-than-wonderful thoughts and feelings take over. Love, more than any other quality, seems to be the most elusive of all, fleeting or fraught with difficulty.

Soul Sailing maintains that because we are spiritual beings sourced and rooted in the Divine, we have Perfect Love already. *In fact, we are Perfect Love.* Perfect Love is the essence of who you are in the highest sense. It is what you experience when you access what we call in this writing, your "Spirit self." This is your true nature. As your Spirit self, you are capable of giving and receiving Perfect Love on a regular basis, on earth, with another person. It is your birthright and your destiny to do so. This is why we say Perfect Love is available to you right here, right now. It is who you are—naturally. Perfect Love need not elude any of us any longer.

To Love Imperfectly

As a spiritual being, you came into this existence on earth in human form with a very special operating system. We like to refer to this as your "Ego Operating System." This is the amazing mental/emotional system within you, the blueprint for what it means to be a human being on a very primitive level. It is not your egotistical self, your self-centeredness, or your inflated self-image, though it may be evidenced as that. Your ego self represents your lower steeped-in-survival self; a self based in ancient, societal needs to live and thrive. It is the voice of fight or flight, protect, defend, judge, be in control, be right. Its job is to keep you safe and in charge in a limited, finite world that is full of insecurity and ripe with danger.

As human beings, we are dominated by our ego selves, its personalities, habits, and desires. We are governed by its emotions. We live minute by minute according to what these emotions tell us: what to think and feel about any given situation, what we like and don't like, what upsets us or makes us feel good, who is right, who is wrong.

In our intimate relationships, the ego especially loves to hold court. You see, when we open ourselves up to meaningful connection with another, especially to love, we naturally become more vulnerable. Our egos, which are rooted in self-protection, become especially active. Because of this, despite how good love may initially feel, the relationship, in time, will likely fall prey to the ego's influence, becoming a roller coaster of emotion, needs, and dissatisfactions—even power struggles—that can result in arguments.

Because we want love so badly, we're willing to do just about anything to make our relationships work. We desperately try to manage our own ego (and its messages), as well as our partner's ego. We struggle with it, trying to wrestle it into submission. Psychological experts tell us that we can bargain, negotiate, compromise, and set boundaries, all of which can improve our intimate relationships. We seem to be saying, "I'll be nice to your ego if you'll be nice to mine." Engaging in this way may provide some relief, but like the champion prize fighter it is, the ego will always rise again and again, ready to engage one more time—to be heard, to be right, and, yes, however misguidedly, even to be loved.

The blueprint for love we have been given at birth, fostered by our collective ego in the guise of culture, is outdated and ineffective. We have been told we can perfect our human selves and thus, perfect our relationships. If we just try a little harder, be a little kinder, love a little more, it will all work out, or so we believe. And yet, despite all of our trying, all of our exploring of various therapies, our attending relationship workshops, and reading countless books on the subject, we remain incredibly frustrated by love. The divorce and infidelity rates continue to rise, our emotional and physical health worsening right along with them. Record numbers of us are taking antidepressants. We remain unhappy, for the most part, with our lives and loves. No surprise. You see, it is impossible to experience Perfect Love with our ego.

Out with the Old, In with the New

But, we can experience Perfect Love through our Spirit selves. A window of opportunity has opened up for us to step away from our old ego way of operating. Please hear us when we say that the ego is not a bad thing. It has kept us safe and powerful for a very long time now. On the flip side, it has also kept us in struggle and unhappiness, disconnected from our true essence, Love, and our Spirit self.

When a new idea dawns upon the horizon, it comes into our consciousness because it is a real possibility—not unlike the use of fire or the ability to fly. We realize we have the capacity to make it part of our reality; otherwise the idea would not have been conceived in the first place. Truly living as our Spirit selves is just such an idea. We propose in this writing that we have gone as far as we can in this human experience embodying our ego selves. Doing so has resulted in thousands of years of human suffering and discord. A next step awaits us. We have shifted in consciousness because we now have the capacity to understand (and activate) what it could mean to live as spiritual beings on this earthly planet. This revolutionary notion can actually change our lives more dramatically than anything we could have previously imagined.

We have now evolved to the point where we can truly choose how we operate in the world—as either our Spirit selves or our ego selves. We can choose the old way or a new way. This may sound deceptively simple, but it's not. Our purpose here is to help you awaken to a new way of living and to create the love and peace-filled existence you have been longing for.

Like never before, we have the power of choice. A new path has opened up for us and we can elect to reorient ourselves toward Spirit and remember how to truly love. We can choose to give and receive love "unconditionally." This means to love without conditions—to love without the ego. This is what we mean by Perfect Love.

Perfect Love is absolutely possible when you choose
to love another as his or her Spirit self.

How can you make this happen? Well, you can begin with learning how to identify whether you are operating as your Spirit self or your ego self at any given moment. Then you can choose a new way to operate—within the "Vibration of Love." In Chapter 2, we'll show you how to get started on your new path to Perfect Love.

Chapter Summary

You are a spiritual being in a human body. You are not your ego or its thoughts or its feelings. Because of a shift in consciousness that has become available to us, we can now choose to live in the world as our Spirit selves and enjoy extraordinary relationships—even Perfect Love. Perfect Love is who you naturally are and what you can experience when you relate to others as your Spirit self, to love them without conditions, without the ego's influence. To do so involves a shift in perception about who you are and how you can relate to others. The Soul Sailing principles and techniques presented here can help you spend more and more time each day living as your Spirit self, bringing you a greater experience of Love, joy, and inner peace.

Reflections

Journal your responses to the following questions:

❧ Notice how your ego is reacting to what you have read so far. What is it saying to you?

❧ Describe any experiences of Perfect Love you might have had in your life up until now. What feelings characterized those episodes?

Listen. Make a way for yourself.
Stop looking in the other way of looking.

JELALUDDIN RUMI

You are love itself—when you are not afraid.

SRI NISARGADATTA MAHARAJ

CHAPTER 2

STAYING ON COURSE: ORIENTING YOURSELF TOWARD SPIRIT

If we wish to arrive at the shores of Perfect Love, we must first orient ourselves toward that destination. In Soul Sailing, just like on the high seas, a compass is important to ensure that we stay on course and don't lose sight of that objective. The compass in this case, however, is not just one instrument, but a variety of tools to help us identify whether we are operating as our Spirit selves or as our ego selves.

Perfect Love resides within our Spirit identity. If we are to fully experience it, we must begin to spend more and more time in our Spirit identity rather than our ego identity.

Look Who's Talking

You are experiencing parts of your Spirit self all throughout the day. Anytime you have a thought or feeling of being kind, caring, generous, or loving, you are operating from your Spirit self. Every positive human quality that we have a name for is part of your Spirit self. Take a moment to review Chart A, "Characteristics of Spirit." You may even have a few more of your own you'd like to add to that list.

31

A.	B.
Characteristics of Spirit	**Characteristics of Ego**
Love	Fear
Peace	Aggression
Oneness	Separation
Happiness	Sadness
Joy	Sorrow
Inner Peace	Anger
Confidence	Insecurity
Abundance	Scarcity
Generosity	Greed
Trust	Suspicion
Appreciation	Cynicism
Hope	Despair
Forgiveness	Resentment
Serenity	Conflict
Compassion	Apathy
Receptivity	Isolation
Optimism	Closed Mindedness
Empowerment	Pessimism
Acceptance	Control
Openheartedness	Judgment
Service	Self-pity

Whenever you have a thought or feeling that ties you up emotionally, causing tension or frustration, you are operating from your ego self. Imagine all the negative qualities we experience as human beings. These are all part of our ego selves. Refer to Chart B, "Characteristics of Ego," and you may recognize these qualities as well.

Because you are a spiritual being having a human experience, you will experience many qualities on both these lists throughout the day. To provide a better understanding of how this dynamic works, we'll use the image of a number line. (See the illustration below.) Left of center on the line is your ego self area of consciousness, and right of center is your Spirit self area of consciousness. At the center, midpoint, your human self will be fading and taking on Spirit qualities. The farther left of center you are functioning, the more your thoughts and feelings will reflect the ego. The farther right of center you are functioning, the more your thoughts and feelings will reflect Spirit.

EGO SELF

| 1 | 2 | 3 | 4 | 5 | 6 | 7 | 8 | 9 | 10 |

SPIRIT SELF

Moment by moment, depending on the experiences you are having, you'll move back and forth on the number line. It reminds us of the lyrics in a Donny and Marie Osmond song, "I'm a little bit country. I'm a little bit rock and roll." We act as if we are a little bit ego and a little bit Spirit. The key to experiencing Perfect Love is to begin to spend more and more time on the higher end of the spectrum—the Spirit end—and to make choices every moment to live and love from this wonderful space. To do so, you just need to identify which foot you are standing on.

Right Foot, Left Foot

Try this simple technique when you need help identifying if you are acting/reacting from Spirit or ego.

When you are feeling badly, experiencing any strong negative emotion, pause, and ask yourself,

Which foot am I standing on?

Let's think of our right foot as our Spirit self and our left foot as our ego self. Identify the feeling you are having:

I'm feeling... (anger, fear, etc.)

If you're asking this question, you are probably standing on your left foot, which represents ego. (If you were standing on your right foot, the Spirit self foot, you would probably not be asking this question in the first place!)

Remember, whenever you feel any of the negative emotions we've listed in Chart B, you have tapped into the energy of your ego self. Once identified, you can decide to remain in that negative energy or to move toward your Spirit self. There are many techniques for doing so, which you'll learn in forthcoming chapters. For now, practice identifying which foot you are standing on and notice how you feel.

Checking In with Yourself

With time and practice, it may not be necessary for you to ask yourself which foot you are standing on. You will simply begin to notice more easily how good or bad you are feeling. By checking in with yourself as often as you can (we recommend several times a day), you can begin to orient yourself more toward Spirit. Just ask yourself a few key questions.

- How am I feeling right now?
- Am I in bliss?
- Am I feeling love and compassion for those around me?
- Is how I feel good enough for me?
- How do I really want to feel?

Notice the emotion that comes up. Is it rooted in your Spirit self or your ego self? Now you are using the compass we spoke of earlier. When you ask questions you are "taking a reading" of how much love and peace you are experiencing at the time. You are getting in touch with your "vibration," the term we use to describe to what extent you are feeling the presence of your

Spirit self and the positive qualities associated with it. With a little bit of practice you can quickly determine where you are on the "vibrational scale" just by checking in with what you are thinking about and how you are feeling. Once you make this assessment, you will know if any action is needed.

Checking in with yourself in this way allows you to determine if you are on course or off. It helps you see where you are headed, either in a negative direction or a positive one, toward ego or Spirit. Check in with yourself—regularly!

Because we human beings have been living, for the most part, as our ego selves, our intimate relationships reflect that. Often they are conflicted and stressful because they are rooted in the characteristics in Chart B. Our desire is to help you identify how you have been operating in the past, and empower you to choose differently, so that your intimate relationships reflect all the qualities of Spirit (Chart A). If you are in a partnership, we recommend checking in with one another often throughout the day. We'll talk more about this in Chapter 5, "Smooth Sailing." It is the best way we know to navigate away from relationship storms.

The Ego Broadcast Network

As human beings, we have an extremely complex operating system. Our human selves consist of both positive and negative thoughts and feelings. As we've discussed, the positive ones reside (for ease of explanation) in our Spirit self, while the negative ones reside in the lower areas of the human consciousness called "ego." Our ego selves are not true conscious selves, but elaborate systems that broadcast their messages out to us. Playfully, we like to call ego the mighty "Ego Broadcast Network."

Just like a radio announcer offers commentary on his program, the ego has its own messages it wants you to hear. Let's take a moment to listen to the commentary your Ego Broadcast Network might be sending you.

> On the surface we hear: *I'm attractive, popular, intelligent, caring, lovable, understanding, successful, peaceful, powerful.*

This is the ego sending broadcasts to build you up to feel (falsely) wonderful about yourself.

> Beneath the surface we hear: *I'm lonely, unhappy, unpopular, not very smart, unskilled, impatient, unlovable, unworthy, overwhelmed.*

This is the ego sending broadcasts to tear you down to feel badly about yourself.

> Underneath it all we might see: *Poor body image, defensiveness, feelings of inadequacy, phoniness, fears, anger, greed, jealousy, hatred, depression, powerlessness, abandonment, invisibility, hopelessness.*

This is the Ego Broadcast Network at its best, bringing up all your insecurities, fears, and old wounds to keep you small and powerless.

On a deeper level we might even hear:
My life is meaningless. I'm crazy. I'm flawed.
My life is a mess. Nothing is ever right.
Everyone is against me. Real love doesn't exist.
The world is a horrible place to be.
Everyone around me is nuts.
I don't want to be here. I hate my life.

This is the ego spiraling wildly, spinning out of control.

Don't despair. These messages are not the *real* you. This "announcer" is only the ego broadcasting to keep you focused away from your Spirit identity. Most of the ego's broadcasted messages are negative, a sure way to keep you disconnected from your truest self. The healthy, positive approach to all of this is to remember that your ego program is perfectly corrupted, a poster child for "program viruses." (See "The Ego: A Computer Program Gone Haywire.")

The ego can even have opposing desires. It appears to be looking out for you, protecting you, but actually it's programmed to keep you separated from others, struggling to satisfy itself, manage, even perfect itself. (This, of course, is an unobtainable and undesirable goal, but the ego doesn't know that, so it will always keep trying.)

The most important step in waking up to the workings of how the human ego program works is to look at ego clearly in the light of day, seeing it for what it is. (See "The Ego: The Wizard Behind the Curtain" on pg. 43.) This will allow you to recognize

The Ego:
A Computer Program Gone Haywire

The technology of computers provides a great model for us to demystify the ego and how it works. I like to think of our egos as a program, a specially created piece of software. By itself, the program has no effect on us. It has no means to display or broadcast its messages. But load it into the human computer (our body with a brain) and off it goes to work on us.

If we have this program running often enough, we'll be prone to its ego messages. Because of its particular energy and the messages it sends, we'll often experience a blow up, or in computer parlance, "a crash." We all know computers do wacky things, but when they do, we don't discard or destroy them. When a crash comes, because we value the computer itself, we try to figure out what caused it. Crashes go with computers, just as speaking through your ego goes with having a human body/mind. The only solution to the problem is to go back and problem solve, trying to figure out what went wrong and vowing to do it differently next time.

We have many choices of what stance we will take with our computers and their programs. For example,

The Ego:
A Computer Program Gone Haywire

many real computers don't like to have multiple programs operating at the same time. It makes them run slow and do strange things. Sometimes by closing every program except what we really need to operate in the moment can be helpful. In this same way, we can choose to turn off any internal computer program that doesn't maximize our positive performance or enhance our relationships. Choose the Spirit program over the ego program and run only that as often as you can!

The best relationship we can have with our human computers is to accept that things will occasionally go haywire, move toward greater understanding of it, and display compassion for ourselves. We can also set an intention to learn more about this operating system and what causes it to freeze or shut down. We don't have to throw our computers out the window just because they're doing what they do best—providing information that can help us learn and grow, even if it's acting up!

⌒ Brad

the previously unimaginable—the ability to choose who you will be in the next moment. There is an alternative to living the messages of the Ego Broadcast Network. You do have choices. Anyone who has the desire to reach for Perfect Love can do just that by choosing Spirit self over ego self.

Remember, that your Spirit self is your direct line to the Divine, to Love. It is God's permanent connection to you and your permanent connection to God. Staying connected with it is how to directly bypass the ego. To bring Perfect Love into your life, you must be ever watchful, always determining which inner world—ego or Spirit—you are operating from at any given moment.

Turning Down the Broadcast, Tuning into Love

To permanently shut off the Ego Broadcast Network is impossible; it will not disappear by your wishing it to do so. And it cannot be annihilated, as some religious teachings imply. As long as you are in a human body, you will have an ego system that begs to be heard. So, how do you deal with it, you might ask. You don't. In fact, you can't, because you cannot change, reason, or bargain with the ego. And you should not try. What you can do is develop a new relationship with it. When your ego wants to be heard, the very best way to relate to it is to simply acknowledge its presence and then turn away from its messages.

This process is very much like listening to a particular station on the radio. When the songs or commentary don't sound good to you, or you tire of listening to it, you change the channel. You can do that with the ego as well. You can literally change the broadcast you're hearing by turning your attention away from it to tune into more appealing sounds, those orchestrated by Spirit. You can tune into a different "vibration."

You see, every thought, word or deed, person, animal or thing has a vibration—an energetic resonance higher or lower, depending where it falls on the scale of life. Your Spirit self has a very high energy or vibration that produces thoughts and feelings of love, peace, and joy. The ego's broadcast has a very low energy or vibration. It contains the lowest of the low notes, those energy-sapping, conflict-producing qualities we've already described.

By using your inner compass (paying close attention to the nature of your thoughts and feelings), you'll begin to recognize these vibrational frequencies—how good or bad they make you feel, how they draw people to you or push them away, how they create harmony or cause conflict. In the next chapter, you will learn how to move away from the influence of the Ego Broadcast Network and its very low vibration, and raise your vibration to the love and peace-filled Spirit range.

∿

Get ready to raise your sails along with your vibration and navigate the seas of your new life. Rest assured, Spirit is guiding the way, even though the waters may feel unfamiliar to you. Trust that Love is calling you home.

The Ego:
The Wizard Behind the Curtain

As a little girl, I loved the movie version of the *Wizard of Oz*. I was envious of Dorothy's ruby slippers, terrified of the Wicked Witch of the West, and completely irritated with the Wizard himself. He seemed like such a fool. Today, as I look at this classic story with different eyes, I can see why that man behind the curtain annoyed me so much. He was a lot like the human ego.

You see, the Wizard of Oz was a fraud. With his booming voice and ferocious image, he had everyone who came to him for a request quaking in their boots. Hidden behind a curtain in the Grand Hall, he was all show and no action, a simple man from the Midwest who had convinced others of his greatness. To protect his status and cover up his insecurities, he remained incognito, pushing and pulling levers that sent out frightening sound effects and ferocious images. He was really afraid and lost, but he certainly did a good job of hiding it. The Wizard was, in many ways, just like our egos.

The Wizard, like the ego, convinced Dorothy and her friends that they did lack certain important qualities: a brain, for intelligence; a heart to love; courage;

The Ego:
The Wizard Behind the Curtain

a sense of home or self. He sent them on a wild goose chase to find the broom of the Wicked Witch, promising them that, upon receiving it, he would reward them with the qualities they desired.

Only by exposing the Wizard did they get wise to his charade. Remember when Toto pulled the curtain back to reveal the Wizard in all his trickery? In the end, Dorothy and her friends realized that they had these qualities within themselves all along. They just had not believed it. A pretend Wizard, just like a false self (ego) had to be exposed for what it was—a big bag of hot air—in order for the friends to wake up to the reality and power of who they really were.

You may enjoy watching the *Wizard of Oz* all over again so you can see how the Wizard/ego likes to operate, keeping us all in fear and insecurity, just like Dorothy, Scarecrow, Tin Man, and Lion discovered by following the yellow brick road.

⇔ Jan

Chapter Summary

You are experiencing parts of your Spirit self and your ego self all day long. You can learn to easily identify which self you are operating from at any given moment in time by checking in with yourself or determining on which "foot" you are standing. By becoming acquainted with the Ego Broadcast Network, the messages it sends, and how they make you feel, you can begin to make positive choices to move away from its influence. Doing so will allow you to have a greater experience of inner peace, happiness, and, ultimately, Perfect Love.

Reflections

Journal your responses to the following questions:

෴ Begin to identify the particular messages that your Ego Broadcast Network likes to regularly send you. What are the top three?

෴ How do the broadcasts make you feel (de-energized, angry, depressed)? Identify how long you usually find yourself staying in that low-vibration energy and how you usually move out of it.

෴ Reflect upon a time when you were very aware of experiencing a high vibration (energy). What were you doing and how did that make you feel?

If I know what Love is, it is because of you.

Come show Yourself
to my soul
in ever—new ways.

Come in scents, come in hues,
come in songs.

Let my body thrill with joy
at Your touch.

RABINDRANATH TAGORE

CHAPTER 3

RAISING THE SAILS: CHOOSING THE VIBRATION OF LOVE

"Vibration" is the term we use to describe to what extent you are feeling the presence of your Spirit self—how much joy, love, peace, compassion, bliss, or any number of Spirit qualities you are feeling in the moment. If these are not present, your vibration is "low" and your ego self is running the roost. If your vibration is high, Spirit is present and thriving. Believe it or not, you do not need to spend any significant time in a low vibration, connected to ego and disconnected from Spirit, no matter how strong the message or sensations might be. You truly have the ability to think and feel higher. You can choose to raise your vibration.

In our Soul Sailing metaphor, raising your vibration is akin to raising the sails of your vessel. With the sails at full mast, raised as high as they can go, you catch the wind of Spirit and move along at remarkable speed. With sails lowered, you creep along in frustration, unable to make much progress toward your destination. A competent Soul Sailor learns how to adjust the sails (vibrations) and harness the power of the wind (Spirit) to arrive at the shores of Perfect Love.

Hear No Ego

We saw a bumper sticker the other day that made an important statement about the power of choice. It said: "You don't have to believe everything you think." Imagine that! The 60,000+ thoughts a day you think—most of them negative—do not have to be accepted or internalized by you. For they are just that—thoughts. They are not facts or even truth. This bumper sticker affirms that we do not need to agree with what the broadcast says to us. We can *hear* it, but we do not have to *listen* to it. There is a difference between hearing and listening.

To have the highest vibration possible will require that you do exactly that—hear. Notice what your ego self is saying to you, but choose not to listen to it or act upon what it says. The moment you begin to listen to the ego's broadcasts, you will feel your positive energy dwindle. The more you listen, the more your vibration will plummet. The beauty of where we are right now in our evolution as human beings is that we have the capacity to choose our thoughts. We can literally say to ourselves, "No, I don't wish to spend time listening to this. I'm choosing to go higher." We simply need to begin doing so on a regular basis.

We are used to our thoughts choosing us instead of us choosing them. When a low-vibration, ego-based thought comes to call, you can focus your attention away from it onto another, more positive one. "Soul Sailing Through Depression" on page 49, "Soul Sailing Through Anxiety," on page 53, and "Soul Sailing Through Pain," on page 57 will give you a better idea of how this process can work in your life with any number of issues. And, in Chapter 5, you will learn specific techniques to refocus your thoughts (individually and as a couple) using high-vibration images.

Soul Sailing through Depression

The most debilitating ego broadcast I have ever experienced came early in the writing of *Perfect Love*. I would wake in the morning to a level of depression that I can only describe as paralyzing. I couldn't move my arms or legs to get out of bed. I would lie there, frozen with my thoughts, stuck in total hopelessness and despair. All the Soul Sailing tools I needed were neatly locked up and out of reach. This paralyzing depression kept me from knowing how to organize my thoughts or grab onto any tools I could use to move forward.

Initially, Jan would talk me through all the great reasons I had for getting up and experiencing another day. Or she'd ask for spiritual help and guidance, sending me healing, loving energy similar to Reiki. It was the combination of her talents and gifts that would bring my vibration to a high enough level to take over the process of raising my vibration the rest of the way. This would often take 45 minutes to an hour of pumping myself full of positive images and thoughts.

Today, when I experience that level of depression, I don't even try to think about steps or tools, I just repeat the phrase "I am Love." With these three simple words my vibration begins to rise right before my eyes and my

Soul Sailing through Depression

morning depression quickly becomes a faint memory. Like many other people, I can awaken to any number of ego broadcasts—from anger to fear to guilt or just plain "I'm not good enough." When I do, I go straight for a "Love Vibration" phrase or word, and in no time I'm again ready to greet the day with an open heart, feeling like my Spirit self.

∾ Brad

Speak No Ego

A similar tactic applies when it comes to *speaking* your ego. You do not have to speak every low-vibration thought that begs to be verbalized. Of course, the ego will do its best to convince you that you should. It will be the source of thoughts like: "I must make my opinion known on this," or "I'm right and they're wrong." It will want you to give voice to all your thoughts and feelings, implying that what is spoken will increase understanding. In fact, the opposite usually occurs. Once you allow the ego to take over, everything goes downhill from there.

The image we like to use to describe this phenomenon is "Ego Abduction." When one of us becomes upset (hooked in by the ego), and is compelled to express our negative feelings, we can expect all kinds of wild things to happen. Words are spoken that we haven't heard before, not to mention behaviors that aren't normally exhibited. It's as if some alien force has abducted the person and taken him or her away, leaving a surrogate behind. The person standing in front of us still looks the same, but what we're witnessing doesn't sound like the person we know and love. This has happened so often to us as a couple over the years that we now jokingly refer to it as an "alien abduction." Somehow labeling it in this way helped us see the ridiculousness of it—and the havoc it wreaked upon our relationship—so we decided to disempower it by calling it what it was. This is another way the ego broadcast tries to get our attention and keep us disconnected from each other and our Spirit selves.

What we've learned through hundreds of our own ego abductions is that it's best if you do not speak through your ego at all.

Simply put, not speaking your ego keeps your vibration high and keeps you operating from your Spirit self.

You can choose any number of traditional techniques to help you not speak through your ego, including: counting to ten before you speak, deep breathing, taking a time-out, and so on. The Soul Sailing method we advocate is:

Speak <u>about</u> your ego, not <u>through</u> your ego.

This powerful technique enables you to disengage from the ego, seeing it as something you experience, not as something you are. To use this method fully requires practice because you may not have been taught to think or speak in this manner. It begins with noticing how you are speaking about your ego-based, low-vibration feelings. When you have the emotion of anger bubble up within you, for example, your natural response is to say, "You make me so mad!" or "I am so angry with you!" That choice of words tells you that you have completely identified with the anger; it has grabbed you and reeled you in, and now you have no choice but to act accordingly. The ego has taken over. You have identified with it and it feels as if this is who you are. Now you are an angry person.

What if you spoke about your anger in a different way? Imagine how much better it could feel if you were to say instead, "I'm experiencing anger." The feeling response within you is now completely different. You are noticing the anger, speaking about it as separate from yourself, and becoming its observer.

It is as if you are taking on the role of a scientist in that moment. You are watching, listening, speaking about what you're

Soul Sailing through Anxiety

For many years I've struggled with anxiety. Any of you who have experienced anxiety know how debilitating and frightening that can be. The episodes ranged from persistent, low-level anxiety to full-blown panic attacks.

One day, in the midst of an extremely bad bout, Brad suggested I try applying Soul Sailing principles. When I felt the symptoms start I could try to be their observer instead of being taken over by them. I did, with Brad's help. He asked me where my thoughts were going minute by minute and how they were making my body feel. As I described them aloud, I sensed myself separating from the symptoms and the episode began to fade. It didn't escalate like it usually did. I was amazed! I became completely calm within just a few minutes.

I next applied the principle of not speaking through my ego to anxiety. I chose not to speak about the anxiety as if it were real and running the show. That way, I would not self-identify with the anxiety. I found myself changing my language completely. I no longer described myself as someone who "had" anxiety, or

Soul Sailing through Anxiety

someone who "suffered" from anxiety. Instead, I would say that I sometimes experienced *feelings* of anxiety. In other words, the anxiety became something I felt once in awhile, but it was not who I was; I was not an anxious person.

This technique also worked with the onset of symptoms. Instead of saying, "Oh, no, it's starting again!" and worrying how far the episode would go, I would say, "I am experiencing a feeling of anxiety." That way I could observe the feeling, not be seduced by it. By pretending I was simply an observer, I could begin to relax, breathe evenly and calmly, and focus my thoughts elsewhere. Within seconds, the anxiousness would dissipate.

This is a method anyone can use for relief of anxiety and a number of other stress-related disorders. We just need to change our minds about the experience and develop a different relationship with it, including the words we speak about it. Words are more important than we realize in creating our reality!

∞ Jan

studying. Doing so puts into motion an entirely different chain of events. You do not experience the intensity of emotion that you would if you claimed that emotion as your own. And because you did not speak from your ego, you did not cause your vibration to severely plummet, causing difficulty between yourself and another person.

Not speaking through your ego is an amazingly powerful tool we'll be sharing in greater depth in Chapter 5. You will be given plenty of opportunity to practice this in the next section, alone and with your partner.

Do What You Love and Love What You Do

Doing something you absolutely love naturally raises your vibration and reorients you toward your Spirit self. You've probably noticed this already. When you are engaged in something you truly enjoy, there is no sense of time or struggle. Perhaps even conscious thought is absent. You are just "being" in the moment. Because each of us is unique, we'll have different activities that raise our vibration. Some examples of vibration-raising actions for you might be:

reading	making love
dancing	being in nature
meditation	listening to music
yoga	cooking
exercising	singing
praying	artistic expression
gardening	bird watching

...any activity or hobby that immerses you in feelings of time-lessness, purposefulness, or inner peace. Engaging in any one of these can raise the energy level of your body, mind, and heart, which in turn fosters thoughts and feelings of well-being. You can also turn to these in an ego emergency, when emotions are running high and you need urgent release. Because we have such positive feelings about our favorite pastimes, they are the perfect Ego Busters!

Take a few moments and create a list for yourself of high-vibration activities. In Chapter 5, "Smooth Sailing," you will be asked to create a couple's list of things you can do together, especially when the two of you are feeling less than wonderful, and wish to stay connected to one another's spirit.

There are also activities that can lower your vibration consid-erably. It is best to avoid them. Alcohol or drug-based activities are prime examples. Initially they may "feel good," but in real-ity, they are depressants that harm your physical and emotional responses. Addictions, in particular, are evidence of a strong ego connection and its powerful hold upon us.

A lower vibration is also created when we are exposed to violent scenarios, whether fabricated (movies and television) or real-life. More and more research is being published about the negative effect of media, even news broadcasts, on our thoughts and emotions. It's important for you to notice how such things impact your vibration and choose to avoid them or counterbal-ance their effects.

Every day we are learning more and more about how our environment affects our vibration. From noise and light, to the food we eat, to the company we keep, the list keeps growing.

Soul Sailing through Pain

In the early nineties, my body was struggling to eliminate kidney stones. It was an excruciatingly painful process. At one point I ended up in the hospital, as the only thing that would cut the pain was shots of morphine or Demerol. But because I was committed to managing my health more holistically, I decided to try a different approach to handling pain.

I can recall one attack in particular, when I went to my bedroom midday, lay down on the bed, and began to intensely focus my thoughts on feelings of peace and love to calm myself. Within minutes, the pain noticeably lessened. During the next hour, I experimented as I lay there, curious to see how well I could affect the intensity of the pain all by myself—honing in on those positive sensations and noting how good I felt, then also noticing how, if I let my thoughts wander, especially back to concern about the pain, the pain would start to get strong again. Back and forth I went until I could regulate the pain to be virtually non-existent and I was able to return to work.

Candace Pert, Ph.D. is a neuroscientist and the author of *Molecules of Emotion: Why You Feel the Way*

Soul Sailing through Pain

You Feel. I recently read her book only to discover that fifteen years ago I was doing what she calls "ecstasy inducing." With the power of thought, I was able to produce enough endorphins to suppress horrendous kidney stone pain. I realize today that what I was doing was raising and lowering my vibration!

She, along with a large number of other researchers, is scientifically proving how thoughts and emotions affect our health, how the body and mind function together in an interrelated system, and that we can positively influence them for enhanced health and peace of mind. Dr. Pert's work confirms what we're saying here—that we really do have a big say in how we feel.

↬ Brad

As you move higher up the vibrational scale, don't be surprised if you become increasingly sensitive to the world around you. The Vibration of Love, of Spirit, is a very high vibration, and when you are exposed to low vibrations, you will begin to feel a dramatic difference in your sense of well-being. As a result, you will be drawn to spend more and more time in the higher vibrations, naturally moving away from situations that don't feel good or aren't Spirit-connected.

Dial 911 for Divine Assistance

Sometimes while Soul Sailing the seas can get rough. The volume of the Ego Broadcast Network is turned up so high you can't seem to hear the voice of Spirit at all. There may be times that you feel frozen, overpowered by the ego's negative messages. No matter how hard you try, no matter how many tools you pull out of your Perfect Love Toolbox, you remain stuck in the mire of that low vibration. You may feel alone, hopeless, or lost. If so, that is the ideal time to dial 911 for Divine assistance.

A direct appeal to your Spirit helpers through prayer or meditation can bring about a dramatic shift in vibration. We have witnessed it ourselves hundreds of times. Call upon the Divine beings with whom you have a personal connection: angels, saints, masters, teachers, a deceased loved one, whomever represents pure and compassionate Spirit presence to you. Everyone has his or her own special way of asking for help. Praying, reciting a rosary, meditating upon an image, chanting, or simply speaking your petition aloud are all viable methods. Use the form that works best for you. In asking for help, it is not so much a Divine intervention that you seek (though that can certainly happen), but a request to realign yourself with the energy of Spirit so you can raise your vibration yourself.

When you invite support in this way, you are sending forth a very powerful intention that says, "I believe Divine assistance is available to me and I am ready to receive it. I intend to feel better and have positive thoughts. I have the desire to raise my vibration."

You can then continue to take action on your own to return to a high-vibration space. You may speak some truths or affirmations that elevate your thoughts: "I am Love" or any "I am . . ." statement affirming your true identity or positive state of being. A personal mantra, word, sound, or image that you have used in meditation can be helpful as well. Repeat this process for as long as you need to feel relief.

Continue to intently focus your thoughts upon how good you *can* feel. Concentrate on the Vibration of Love and imagine what that feels like. Observe your overall vibration and visualize it, feel it inching slowly upward. Notice how much lighter you feel, how much brighter everything looks. The more focused you can be, obviously, the faster your vibration will rise back into the Spirit range.

Never doubt the power of the "heavens" to influence your earthly journey. You are not meant to do this journey alone. If a human partner is not available to lend a helping hand during turbulent ego times, rest assured, celestial ones are. Calling upon them and pairing their efforts with your own vibration-raising ones is a powerful combination, one that the ego cannot defeat, no matter how hard it tries.

Spirit Walks

Maintaining a high vibration can feel at times like one big roller coaster ride, a series of ups and downs that never seem to end. This is because there are significant gaps between the times when you experience a high vibration. Life happens, crises arise, and it is easy to get carried away into low-vibration responses. If you ignore your vibration long enough, have added stress, or feel certain issues pressing upon you, your vibration will inevitably slip back toward the ego realm in no time. We are not used to maintaining a consistently high vibration. It has not yet become a day-to-day habit with us, much less a lifestyle.

If you're wondering if it's possible to hold your Spirit vibration on a more permanent basis, the answer is yes—with time and practice. You see, Soul Sailing is very much like learning to walk. As children, when the innate urge to move independently kicked in, we had to learn to crawl first. Then, we took those initial faltering steps, but we were down on the floor more than we were up walking. It takes a tremendous effort to hold one's balance while standing, let alone moving about on two legs. Up and down, up and down we went. Our whole body/mind system had to come together to perform the function of walking on two sturdy legs without faltering.

The same is true for learning how to operate as our Spirit selves. It takes practice, time, and a Divine readiness of body, mind, and spirit coming together in exactly the right way to make it happen. A day will come, however, when we'll view living as our Spirit selves as a totally natural act, just as we can now walk without consciously trying.

From another perspective, humans have always crawled through life. From this moment on, we have the choice to move through our days in a new way. We will begin to witness others starting to walk upright as they begin operating as their Spirit selves. As time goes on, more and more people will realize it's far easier than they realized, and much more beneficial and enjoyable to stroll through life as Spirit. We believe it will become commonplace to do so. Crawling cannot possibly take us where we want to go any longer.

The Slinky Effect

As human beings, we are creatures of habit. We keep doing the same things over and over again and hope the outcome will change. With Soul Sailing, we are stretching ourselves beyond where we have ever gone before. But our human operating system, especially the Ego Broadcast Network, is very strong, so it's inevitable that it will try to pull us back into habitual ways of thinking and old behaviors. Established patterns die hard.

Our human operating system is very much like a Slinky. The more you exercise it, use it, stretch it into new directions and dimensions, the more room it has to expand. The gaps between the rings of a Slinky get wider and wider with increased use, until there is actually significant space between them. A well-used Slinky never totally goes back to the way it was. Our system is "hard-wired" with a Slinky-like effect to act and respond the same way time and again. But, if we give it a good workout, it does change and we change. It just takes time and plenty of useful practice.

We're here to tell you not to be surprised when your former buddy, the ego, snaps back into your day-to-day life just like that Slinky. It's only doing what it does best—going back to what is familiar, trying to retake its shape. But that's alright, because YOU are growing and changing. YOU are developing a new relationship with the ego. YOU are taking one small step after another to leave your ego self behind and live the life you were meant to live as your highest spiritual self.

Cultivating Compassion

As a couple, we often laugh about the ego and its wiliness, its cunning, its outright audacity, and all the crazy methods it uses to retain its influence over us, trying to keep us disconnected from our Spirit selves and each other. It amazes us how hard ego labors sometimes, working to convince us that WE are the crazy ones! Because of this, it's best to keep a lighthearted tone about this whole process. We need not take ourselves, especially our ego selves, so seriously.

The fact of the matter is, the ego will never give up the fight to be in the forefront, to be in control. It will always show up to play, even though you hope it won't, just like the bully in the school yard. And because it does, you will be asked repeatedly throughout your day, even second by second, to choose Spirit over ego, to select a higher vibration for yourself.

There is no way to annihilate the ego or make it go away for good. There is only one way to loosen its iron grip on you—by exercising the most powerful Spirit quality of all—compassion. You can cultivate compassion for the ego because it is so insecure, rooted in fear; compassion for others because they are struggling with their egos, just as you are; compassion for yourself because, in your humanity, you will fall prey to the ego again and again. It is inevitable to do so, no matter how hard you practice the principles shared here or how adept you become at using the tools in your Perfect Love Toolbox. The ego self will always be present because it holds the blueprint for what it means to be a human being. We cannot exist in a body without it.

Fortunately, the ego cannot stand up long to compassion. It is the highest vibration we can hope to access—the vibration of unconditional Love. It sends a message to the receiver (either ourselves or another) that says, "I love you, no matter what. I love you without judgment. I love you simply because you are. And what you are is Spirit."

When you can access the compassion that naturally exists within you, the ego begins to melt away. A high vibration of compassion can dissolve any ego thoughts and the emotions tied to them. A low vibration cannot exist at the same time as our most dominant Spirit thought. It is simply impossible.

That is why we say Perfect Love is right here, right now. It is available to you as soon as you choose its vibration for yourself.

When you feel compassion for yourself as a spiritual being having a human experience, and compassion for another who is doing the same, you will begin to experience Perfect Love.

Your course has been set and the sails raised to catch the breezes of bliss—the Vibration of Love. Who shall your Soul Sailing companions be and how do you journey into Perfect Love with them? In Chapter 4, you will learn how wonderful life can be when you and your partner begin this quest to your highest selves—together.

Chapter Summary

You can hear the messages of the ego, but you can choose not to listen to them. You can also learn not to speak your ego, to give it voice, but instead speak "about it." This will help you become its observer and move away from its influence. Any number of techniques are available to raise your vibration out of the ego range into the Spirit range, including: engaging in an activity you love, avoiding vibration-lowering activities, and asking for Divine assistance. Cultivating compassion for yourself and others is one of the highest vibration-raising practices you can engage in, one that naturally creates experiences of Perfect Love.

Reflections

Journal your responses to the following questions:

- Practice "speaking Spirit" with a friend or partner. Choose one ego thought and observe it. Notice how different you felt when you spoke this way. How did the listener feel hearing you speak like this? Discuss your responses together.

- Reflect upon any situations, people, or activities where you have noticed a large energy drop in your positive (Spirit) vibration. How might you better respond to those in the future?

❧ What is the degree to which you are feeling compassion for yourself or others right now? Reflect upon why this might be so and what vibration-raising activity you could engage in to shift it.

*The minute I heard my first love story
I started looking for you, not knowing
how blind that was.*

*Lovers don't finally meet somewhere
They're in each other all along.*

JELALUDDIN RUMI

*It is right and necessary that we should be individuals.
The Divine Spirit never made any two things alike—
no two rosebushes, two snowflakes,
two grains of sand, two persons.*

*We are all just a little unique for each wears a different
face; but behind each face is One Presence—God.*

ERNEST HOLMES

CHAPTER 4

NAVIGATING LIFE'S SEAS: SOUL SAILING WITH YOUR BELOVED

Some may think the best way to connect with your Spirit self is by being alone, escaping from society, or moving anywhere you can singularly experience the Divine without distraction. While it is true that you can enhance your Spirit connection through solitude, the simple act of being in intimate partnership will do so as well, perhaps with even more profound and powerful results.

The great wise ones who have gone before us, from Jesus to Buddha, did not isolate themselves to seek God. Though they spent important time in solitude, they returned to the world of human relationships to show us firsthand how to be Love's presence to one another. They knew that when we are with other people, we will also encounter the Divine within ourselves, and the Divine One in every other person. They encouraged us, by their own examples, to "Be Love."

It's All About You

With every human interaction, no matter what the relationship, intimate or casual, you are being given the unique opportunity to see which self you are operating from at any given moment—your Spirit self or your ego self. When the primary companion on your Soul Sailing journey is your intimate partner, you can safely embark on a sacred voyage of personal discovery. Now you can learn, once and for all, who you really are, as an individual and as a couple, and uncover your ability to give and receive Perfect Love.

How does this process occur? It begins quite unknowingly, subtly. Your partner will act in a certain way and you'll respond accordingly. For example, when one party expresses anger, the other can choose to respond back with anger or to offer another response altogether. It may not feel as if you have a choice because your ego will immediately attempt to draw you in. In fact, you do have a wide range of choices available to you.

Every interaction, no matter what the situation, whether it is a subtle irritating habit or an outright behavior that disturbs you, will bring you to a moment of reckoning. Now you can decide which version of yourself you wish to be. In a matter of seconds, you can stop and take a mental snapshot of yourself. You can see on which foot you are standing (right foot/Spirit; left foot/Ego) and how low or high your vibration is.

In your intimate relationship, this will be especially pronounced because you are so deeply connected to this person. Everything your partner does or says can affect you. However, being in relationship is not really about being in relationship with another—it is about being in relationship with *yourself*. Every word you hear, every action you observe, provides *you* with an opportunity to react, to feel a particular emotion, or think a certain thought. Undoubtedly, others will do things to irritate you—to "push your buttons," so to speak. Therein lies the secret. These are *your* buttons, not theirs. By being in relationship, you get to watch *your* reaction, and to experience *your* response to them.

Here's some news for you: being in relationship is not about changing your partner so you will feel more comfortable. That is only more ego-managing behavior. Underneath each button they push is an issue you now have an opportunity to look at, if you are ready and willing. This is why intimate partnership is so very important to our spiritual journey. Simply by being in relationship with that special someone, you get to see all your human ego "stuff." And believe us, each of us has a lot of stuff we bring along for the ride of relationship! The beauty of this process is that you get to release it with your partner, the one who loves you unconditionally, ego warts and all. And you get to do the same for him or her.

Your Soul's Companion

Your relationship partner has come into your life to help you uncover your ego self, make choices about it, and move toward a higher version of who you really are. This is why it has often been said that relationships are mirrors. If you have committed to your own growth journey with another, you will get to experience every emotion possible and then be given the opportunity to take a good look at yourself in the mirror of your relationship. You will be asked to look at why you react and feel the way you do. You will be asked to uncover and expose all of your fears. You will be asked to let go of everything that holds you back from being your most Divine self, to heal old wounds, to let go of ego mechanisms, and to live more fully as your Spirit self.

From the moment of our birth into this world as human beings, we experience many negative things, as well as many positive ones. Because of those experiences we develop certain qualities or personality traits—both negative and positive. Within each of us is the darkest of the dark and the lightest of the light. When we begin to have an awareness that we are not just tragically flawed human beings, but Divine ones having a human experience, we realize that we need to release all the dark parts of ourselves so we can have a greater experience of Spirit. Our relationships do just that for us.

Your partner is the person who is here at this juncture to help you move to a higher level of being. Some people refer to this person as a "soul mate," but we prefer to use the term "soul companion." A soul mate implies that there is only one individual who can fit this bill. In actuality, you may have many soul mates—or soul companions—because anyone you engage in a relationship, who helps you grow spiritually, is just that—a companion to your soul's growth. That is why the person is here in your life, playing that role—to escalate your growth. And you are here to escalate his or hers.

Of course, we are never guaranteed the outcome of our relationship encounters. We each have free will. We each have choices to make about whether we will grow or remain static. We never quite know how we will grow when we're in a relationship, but despite the outcome, we are given a great gift by its presence in our lives.

Soul Sailing constantly challenges us to evolve within our relationships, to learn and grow individually and together. Because of this, we are in a continuous state of enlightenment.

Every encounter is a sacred encounter. If you are aware that you are your Spirit self, then every relationship offers you an opportunity to learn something new about yourself. Every relationship will unlock ego-based issues that are important for you to look at, leave behind, or make peace with. Your relationship, therefore, becomes the vessel by which you move into deeper awareness of yourself, your spirit, and God.

Your Soul Sailing Creed

To experience Perfect Love with one another, you will need to build your intimate connection upon one all-important principle:

We enter into this relationship as two spirits, not two egos.

You will also need to set a very powerful intention that states:

We will live and operate as Spirit.
We will love each other as our Spirit selves.

With these acknowledgments, you can immediately enter into a new type of relationship. Together, you can avow that you've come to this relationship for the highest purpose possible: to be your highest selves and to connect with the divine essence found within one another.

Soul Sailing proposes a series of powerful relationship principles. These are written like a creed. We invite you to discuss them and allow them to form the "Foundation" of your Spirit-led relationship. With this credo in place, nothing can weaken your Foundation; no amount of ego interaction, and no degree of personal, familial, or societal challenges can disable or destroy it.

The Soul Sailing Creed

We agree that we do not desire to be in an ego-based relationship.
We desire a new and different experience of love.
We agree upon who we are to one another.
We are partners. We are united and One.

Our Foundation also recognizes that each of us possesses
a very powerful human operating system, or ego self,
which accompanies us into relationship. But this is not who we
truly are and it is not part of our Foundation.
The ego's presence may result in differences of opinion,
even arguments, but it does not define our relationship.
No matter what circumstances befall us, no matter how badly
our egos act out, we remain connected to each other because
our Foundation is solid and strong.
This never changes.

Together we are growing into higher versions of ourselves.
Together we are Spirit.
Together we are Love.

In our own lives as Soul Sailing partners, we affirm these precepts again and again. We remind each other of them, especially when challenges arise. When one of us is struggling, we renew our commitment to our relationship by remembering who we are to one another. It is only through our deep commitment to ourselves and to our Foundation that we have weathered the stormy seas of human relationship. We know, as Spirit beings in human bodies, that ego disruptions will happen, despite all our good intentions and relationship skill building.

Love Will Keep You Together

Your togetherness, your bond, is truly what will keep your Foundation intact. When you realize that you are two spirits having a human experience *together*, then your relationship can focus upon how you can best help one another grow and become more attuned to Spirit. Your focus is not on your differences, but on your similarities of experience, the common experience of having a beautiful, new relationship.

There is no true sense of partnership in ego-based relationships because each ego is trying its best to be heard, to be right, or to be in charge. There is no sense of oneness. Instead, the relationship is characterized by two egos having a "battle of the personalities." The ego will always try its best to be in control, setting us apart from each other, making one right and one wrong. In time, we become adversaries, rather than partners.

As a Soul Sailing couple, even when you have disagreements, your Foundation can keep your partnership intact. You can frame your disagreements differently. In the midst of an ego tussle, you do not have to lose sight of your mutual purpose: to be your Spirit selves to one another and to love one another accordingly. You know that any difficulties that arise will *not* destroy your Foundation. In fact, they can strengthen it, because with every ego disagreement comes an opportunity to heal, to let go, and to love from a deeper place within you ... to love one another as your Spirit selves.

Come Home to Your Beloved

Soul Sailing will challenge you to increase your ability to give and receive love as Spirit. Your partner's presence offers you the opportunity to "be love" and to "be loved." Thus the word, "Beloved." Loving is the highest form of activity a human being can engage in. This wonderful person you have formed a bond with is your Beloved and you are his or hers.

In order to be someone's Beloved, however, you must first be the Beloved to yourself. You cannot possibly give to another what you have not given to yourself. As a spiritual being, you have unconditional love within you, simply by the nature of your birth. Even if you believe you have never personally experienced it, nor received it from another human being, don't despair. Your capacity to love unconditionally is very present, even if it has not been a felt experience in your lifetime. This is because Love is your source. It is who you are at your core.

Your intimate relationship will help illuminate your "Love Quotient," your current ability to give and receive Love. Trust that the beautiful partnership you have entered into will help you tap into that vast storehouse of Love within you. Your Beloved is here, and you can help him or her access unlimited Love for self, for each other, and for everyone with whom you both come in contact. But, how do you make yourselves available to unconditional Love if you have never experienced it?

What's Your Love Quotient?

Being in relationship with another will offer you daily opportunities to check your Love Quotient: the measure of your current ability to give and receive Love. Check your Love Quotient by making an honest assessment of how openhearted or closed down you are feeling in any given moment. Are you desiring to embrace and be embraced? Or are you feeling more like a wounded animal who wants nothing more than to slink off to its corner and be alone?

Does this process sound familiar? It should. It's just another way to check your vibration. By asking yourself "How much Love am I really feeling right now?" you have a good, clear indicator of where you are on the vibrational scale.

This is especially helpful when your partner is feeling prickly or short-tempered. You can be an ego observer, and choose not to be drawn into any negative energy. Before you respond to any words or actions, you can ask yourself two very important Love Quotient questions:

How would Love respond?

or

What is the loving thing to do in this situation?

What's Your Love Quotient?

Within the time it takes to breathe in a few, quick, centering breaths, you can quickly determine your current Vibration of Love, then choose to respond as Love would—with kind words, caring gestures, and, most important, compassion—the highest form of Love available to all of us. Assessing our Love Quotient in this way allows us to once more "Be the Love" we are and can be in the world, especially in this moment, to our partner, who is struggling to remember the same thing.

The answer is simple. When you acknowledge that you are one another's Beloved, you naturally move into the higher Vibration of Love. This vibration is very different from the feeling of falling in love or being in love. It is also different from showing or demonstrating love to someone. As Beloveds, you embody the true spirit of the Hindu term "Namasté:" the Spirit in me acknowledges and honors the Spirit in you. As we understand its meaning, Namasté was a greeting used by Hindustanti pilgrims as they hiked through the Himalayas. If their paths crossed, they would stop and bow, and say Namasté to one another, a salutation of honor, respect, and appreciation for that person and his or her journey.

Through intimate partnership, you can truly learn how to "be Love" to another individual, maybe for the first time in your life. Your relationship can mirror and embody the greatest Love of all—Divine Love—the presence of Spirit in and around us. We *can* be God to one another, God in human form with eyes and ears and wide open hearts big enough to Love us into the grandest version of who we can be on this planet Earth.

Discovering Your Relationship Truths

The word "Truth" implies that there are solid principles, timeless ideas of what is right or good for all of us. As soul companions uncovering Perfect Love, you will find yourselves unearthing your own set of "relationship Truths" as a couple. These are ways of being with one another—how you speak, relate, and connect which nurture and support your loving relationship. By setting the intention to be your highest selves with one another, very gradually you will discover your Truths. For each couple, this will vary. The longer you are in relationship, the more these will be revealed.

And that is the key—*revealed*. Soul Sailing is an organic process, one that allows our natural state of being Spirit to emerge. You will also discover, by trial and error, many more actions that will pull you away from one another. When they do, you will learn to identify them as ego broadcasts and later avoid them at all costs.

One such example is sarcasm. In the early days of our own relationship, we learned that using a certain tone, one laden with sarcasm, was highly destructive, even if offered in humor. It made us shut down immediately and feel very hurt. We explored this together to discover why we did this hurtful thing, but in the end, it really didn't matter what that source was (just another ego defense mechanism). What did matter was that we got in touch with one of our relationship Truths. We learned that using sarcasm did not foster feelings of love between us. We then "intended" to always try to speak to one another in ways that enhanced our Spirit connection. You will discover your own Truths, as we did, if you listen deeply to one another from your Spirit selves. These Truths will be revealed to you, organically, by your unique life situations.

There are no rules, dictates, or expectations in Perfect Love other than the commitment to operate from Spirit as much as possible. There are many books for couples that present a set of rules for how to behave with one another, but these are not necessary if you hold true to your Foundation, and agree to operate as best you can as Spirit. Because your Foundation is unshakable

Seeing Your Partner as Sacred

Sometimes it's hard to imagine how we could possibly vibrate at a high enough vibration to experience others as pure Spirit. How can we unconditionally love anyone, especially with the Ego Broadcast Network bombarding us with messages fraught with judgment and opinions? An exercise in having "sacred vision" works wonders toward this end.

Imagine for a moment that you have put on a pair of special eyeglasses that enable you to see each person in a new way. The glasses are comfortable and light to wear. They have the effect of revealing the person in front of you with soft eyes, much like one of those special movie filters used years ago to make Hollywood starlets look even more beautiful than they were. When you look through these lenses, you see the unique way that Spirit has come into the world in the form of this particular human being. You can marvel at the ingenuity required to make each person such a unique rendering of Spirit.

Offer a quick prayer of gratitude for him or her and the distinct role he or she has been brought here to play in the world. Now, take your glasses off and

Seeing Your Partner as Sacred

notice how you view this person. Does the effect of your soft-focus lenses linger? Are you experiencing more love and compassion in your heart?

Reflect for a moment on what life might be like if we could strive to see our fellow travelers, especially our partner, with Jesus' or Buddha's eyes, with sacred vision.

and because you have set the highest intentions for your relationship, you will be shown the way. If you have faith and trust the process at work, you will naturally be taken to where you need to go. You don't have to "handle" or manage each other or your relationship. Love, with a capital L, will guide you.

Imagine for a moment how different it would feel if the person you are in intimate relationship with was your Beloved. How would you treat him or her? How would you speak to this very special person? When in doubt, revisit the qualities presented in Chapter 2, Chart A, and you will see how well you are aligned with Spirit in your interactions. If the way you are communicating results in the feelings presented in Chart B, you'll know you need to revisit your choice of words, looks, or touches and move back into the arena of Spirit.

There is an attitude of reverence that builds when you realize you have been paired with an individual who conveys the highest source of earthly Love for you. Imagine the joy and gratitude you would feel day in and day out for this person in your life. You really can be someone's Beloved and they can be yours. In fact, you already are. You just need to shift how you perceive one another and, especially if you are already in a committed relationship, start to treat each other accordingly.

What an amazing gift we have been given in human relationship! What a privilege it is to journey with someone in this way and be part of the unfolding of their Divine nature. As your voyage continues, you will grow in appreciation and gratitude for one another as loyal traveling companions. You will naturally wish to keep your connection strong.

In Part II, you will learn many, many ways that the two of you can cultivate your sacred connection and keep your relationship on an even keel, no matter where the seas of life take you.

Chapter Summary

Your intimate relationship can offer you a profound path of awakening—a journey to your Spirit self. Your partner is here as a soul companion to help you uncover the ways in which you continue to operate as your ego self and to support you as you move into a greater experience of Spirit. The "Soul Sailing Creed" can help the two of you stay focused in who you really are to one another, and is the basis of an unbreakable bond, your Foundation, which will carry you through the highs and lows of your relationship lessons. Your partner is also your Beloved, a representative of the Divine, who invites you to remember how Love can really be. Together you create a larger third energy, a true manifestation of Divine energy made visible in the world.

Reflections

Journal your response to the following questions:

ॐ Think about a time when another person "pushed your buttons" and you realized it was not about them, but about you and your issue. How did the situation play itself out?

∾ Have you had a previous experience of someone being your soul companion, i.e., you knew that they were in your life to spur on your own growth? Describe that relationship and where it brought you in terms of your life journey.

∾ At this moment, what would you assess your Love Quotient to be? Why?

Part II

The Perfect Love
Toolbox

There is nothing like making love with the Beloved.
Nothing like the boundary-less heart
to make us edgeless and agile.

STEPHEN AND ONDREA LEVINE

The secret of Love is creativity.
Lovingly tend your relationship like a garden.
Keep it seeded with fresh interests, fresh ideas,
that grow always more beautiful.
Weed it, lest the flower beds overrun with weeds
of unconscious habits. For love to be ever new,
it must be approached with creativity, as an art.

J. DONALD WALTERS

CHAPTER 5

SMOOTH SAILING:
LOVE LINKS

Together you can set the intention to stay connected to one another as your Spirit selves. You'll want to do so to stay in the flow of Love and to keep your vibration high.

By exploring and implementing these "Love Links," and creating more of your own, you will enhance the day-to-day quality of your relationship and circumvent conflict. Your relationship will deepen in intimacy, passion, and trust when your daily life together is not a roller coaster of emotions, and you're not thrown off center managing one ego crisis after another. In fact, nothing can wear out a beautiful relationship more than the continued stress of engaging in damage control.

Staying connected by using the techniques presented here will help you avoid the stormy seas of relationship and keep your love boat on an even keel.

LOVE LINK 1

SPEAK SPIRIT!

Communicate with one another using Spirit language, rather than the language of the Ego Broadcast. This is a big shift in communication style for any couple. Until now, you have probably been speaking as if you *are* the feelings you're experiencing. "I *am* angry. I *am* jealous." To begin to "speak Spirit" you must be vigilant about observing the ego's messages and choosing not to speak them aloud or act upon them, especially to your partner. You can speak *about* the feelings: "I am experiencing some feelings of anger" or "My ego is sending messages of jealousy." This is the language of Spirit. To speak those feelings as if they *are* you, is to speak your ego.

The effect of speaking to one another in this way is powerful. It allows you to separate yourself from the strong emotions that are trying to surface. It also does not make your partner wrong for having done something to cause a strong reaction in you. You are not pointing a finger at your partner or blaming him or her, which keeps the two of you in alignment.

Speaking *about* your ego enables you both to witness the ego and join efforts to resist its pull. You remain connected, jointly committed to observing any ego episode. In this way, you are true partners to one another, instead of adversaries.

Practice speaking Spirit together. The more you do it, the easier it will become. As a couple you can assist each other with this. You can point out how the ego may be trying to take over. You can gently say to one another, "Don't forget. You have some choices. You have some tools." Do so with love and compassion for one another.

LOVE LINK 2

REMEMBER THE LOVE

The two of you fell in love for a reason: to companion one another on your journeys to connect with your Spirit selves. In that, you are one another's Beloved.

If you find yourself beginning to feel distant from one another, take time to "remember the Love." Recall your first meeting, your initial attraction, the thrill you felt in the early stages of your relationship. Reflect upon the unique gifts of your relationship and the great goodness it has brought into your lives. Offer thanks for its awakening presence.

Check in with yourself also—regularly—to determine how you are treating your partner. Are you treating him or her like your Beloved? Are you nurturing, supportive, a good listener? Are you feeling generous toward him or her? Compassionate?

Your ego self will naturally want to focus in on what's wrong in your relationship, not what's right. It will want to spotlight your partner's irritating qualities and what is lacking. This is what a human ego does best: it tries to separate the two of you, making your partner seem less desirable, even wrong for you. It will take conscious effort on your part to rise above such thinking and remember why you have come together, to grow, to move beyond the ego connection and experience Perfect Love. Accept the fact that your ego will try to manipulate you to believe your relationship is less than perfect. Connect with your Spirit self and your partner's Spirit self as often as you can. Remember who you are to one another.

LOVE LINK 3

SIT HIGHER UP IN THE BLEACHERS

Taking the time to view your relationship from a higher perspective can be very helpful in maintaining a strong connection. You can do this by sitting higher up in the bleachers.

Using the metaphor of a football game, imagine yourselves sitting in the first row, where all you can see are the players, bodies in uniforms crashing into one another. You're not really sure what's happening, as everything's a blur of movement when you're seated so near the activity. Move up higher in the bleachers and you can see the entire playing field. You can watch the maneuvers, the progress, the losses, and the victories. Your relationship is much like that football game. When you are so close to the action, it's difficult to see what's really going on.

It's important that you keep in mind the bigger picture of your relationship, from a spiritual perspective. Doing so is a vibration-raising act in itself. When your vibration is high and you're viewing your relationship through Spirit eyes, you can see your day-to-day interactions as the learnings they are. Take time to reflect upon how you are still getting caught up in certain ego broadcasts. It's ideal to do this both alone and together. Look for the ego maneuvers and see how it invites you to be a player.

Take time to reflect upon how you're growing as individuals. Note your progress as a couple. Ask yourselves how well you're doing as Soul Sailors.

Being observers from as high up in the bleachers as you can go helps you see your "ego plays" and the fouls. Every time you stop and engage in this process, your vibration as a couple will rise. Your connection deepens. Applaud your growth and set new intentions to build upon what you've learned.

LOVE LINK 4

LOVING TOUCH

Nurture your physical connection and keep it strong. Loving touch, whether passionate or tender, is one of the most important ways to enhance your connection. Your physicality is not separate from your spirituality. In fact, we often experience the Divine, and our partner as the Beloved, through our senses: touch, sound, sight, and smell. The body is the primary vehicle through which we have a "felt" experience of what it means to be loved.

When you are operating as your Spirit self, you naturally outpour love and affection to others through kind, compassionate words or through loving touch: kissing, hugging, or making love. Both giving and receiving love in these ways raises your vibration. It is only your ego self that withholds affection and kindness. It is your ego that stifles passion and excitement.

Use your physical connection as a centering exercise. If you are feeling distant, lie down together in a comfortable place side by side, holding hands. Relax and take deep breaths together. This can re-establish your connection, helping you remember who you are together. Feel the energy begin to shift toward the positive. In this way, you connect with your partner's energy field. The human aura can expand to about ten feet, so to deepen your connection, get close—the closer the better.

Intimate physical contact can also move us toward feeling a sense of Oneness. If your body/mind/spirit connection is especially deep at any given moment, you may feel no separation at all, but a gentle blending of your bodies, as if your skin and bones have disappeared and there is no difference between the two of you. This is a profound experience and one that many couples report when high-vibration states are reached simultaneously.

Eye contact can deepen your physical intimacy as well, and draw you toward one another. It has been said that the eyes are the window of the soul. Focusing on the soul behind your partner's eyes can rekindle your memory of why this person is your Beloved.

LOVE LINK 5

SHOW AND TELL

Offer loving words and gestures to one another. As a couple you can form agreements about using loving communication as a part of your Foundation. For example, sarcasm is not a compassionate way to express one's self to your Beloved. You can agree to speak with one another without that element present. You can also agree not to verbally attack, insult, or mock one another. These are very low-vibration communication qualities.

It is perfectly acceptable to discuss these things as your relationship begins and set some intentions to speak lovingly. The way you talk to one another truly is a matter of choice. Egos attack, Love doesn't. Egos yell and scream, Love doesn't. Set the intention to follow the course set by Spirit and choose the loving response again and again.

You will find that when your vibration is high, when you are operating as your Spirit self, speaking and acting lovingly is natural. You do not want to do it any other way. It is a manifestation of the true Love, joy, and compassion you're feeling inside.

LOVE LINK 6

MEDITATE TOGETHER

Sit side by side in meditation to raise your vibration together. This can be done in any number of ways:

- ⮞ Select and focus on an image together. Create a joint list of possible symbols, pictures, or memories you share that hold a high vibration for the two of you—activities you enjoy doing together, places you have been, and things, and qualities that are important to you.

- ⮞ Choose a phrase or mantra that you repeat silently together. Some ideas are: "I am Love," "We are Love," "We are One," and "I am peace," etc.

ᵱ Select your own personal image or mantra to focus on, for each of you may have unique formulas that raise your vibration. For example: one of you might be particularly drawn to nature images, the other to words or symbols.

You can think of these mental getaways as mini-vacations you take with one another. If you keep going back to these "places" in your meditation time, you will continually nurture your relationship and restore connection if it has become distant.

Meditating together can also enhance your creativity. It can deepen your ability to listen to your inner workings, as well as to listen more effectively to your partner. It can provide insights into lessons you are learning together, and offer tips and tools that you can use as a couple to stay connected or overcome difficulty. It opens you up to greater healing, both personally and as a couple.

Of course, meditating is also another wonderful way to tap into the Oneness that you are. You can lose any sense of separateness when you join your energies in this way. What a beautiful way to spend quality time together!

LOVE LINK 7

DO WHAT YOU LOVE

Create a list of all the things you enjoy doing together as a couple. Do you recall the list you created for yourself in Chapter 3? What are your commonly shared interests and hobbies? What are you both passionate about? You've probably noticed that when you are sharing these special times together, you feel amazingly good. That's because your individual vibrations and your connection as partners is very high when you are doing what you both love.

To stay connected, engage in these activities on a regular basis. They form a very important bond between you and they nurture your partnership, so be sure to make time for them. When they are neglected because of inattention or busyness, you will certainly feel the effects—a low vibration or feelings of edginess with one another. Some days, staying connected does take special effort, and you will need to consciously choose things to do to elevate your vibration as a couple.

Keep your list handy, perhaps tucked inside the pages of this book, because you will be referring to it later on in Part II—"Coming Back Together" after a relationship storm.

LOVE LINK 8

CREATE SACRED SPACE

Do the two of you have a special place set aside where you can relate on a higher level? With all that can distract you or lower your vibration on a daily basis, an established sacred space can support your connection with one another. This can be a bedroom, den, or meditation room.

Examine the energy of this room and become aware of its ability to intensify or to erode your connection. Your bedroom may be the best place for this, so take the time to make it invitational and nurturing. Create a supportive atmosphere for lovemaking. Jointly choose items and furnishings that promote feelings of peace and love. Remove clutter, piles, and unwanted items and add elements of comfort through color, aromatherapy, candles, and music. Make this a special place for the two of you to go to remember your Oneness.

Maintaining this space is just as important as creating it. Jointly make your bed together. Keep it tidy and teeming with positive energy. (Clear out negative energy when needed, especially after a disagreement of any sort.) Keep it current by introducing new items (decor) of meaning to you both. These actions create a positive intention, which reminds you that the space you share is an important part of who you are together and that you desire to grow in intimacy.

LOVE LINK 9

CHECK IN WITH EACH OTHER

Agree to take time daily to check in with each other and see how you're feeling, noting the level of your vibration at that moment. First thing in the morning, at day's end, or anytime you might notice your partner struggling with ego are ideal opportunities to connect with him or her. Checking in sends the strongest possible messages of love and support to your partner, messages of "I care about you," and "I am here for you," "We're in this together." This, maybe more than any other Love Link, will allow you to experience Perfect Love.

Using Spirit talk (Love Link 1), encourage your partner to share his or her thoughts and feelings. Remember, that by asking, you are opening yourself up to another growth experience; another opportunity to observe your Ego Operating System, to talk about what the broadcast is saying and how it's making you feel. It invites you to be a true partner as well, to listen with an open heart and to "hold a space" (Ego Buster 9) for you both to learn and grow.

Checking in also prevents toxic buildup in your relationship. The ego loves to hold onto hurts and disappointments and pile them one on top of another to create a huge tower of negative feelings. We call this "stacking." It's as if the ego is making a case for itself, gathering evidence to prove a point or right a perceived wrong. When you check in with each other on a daily basis, stacking is much less likely to happen. Misperceptions can be immediately examined so your connection remains strong.

You can also check in by asking yourselves "How are WE doing?" Take time to discuss impressions of how you are doing as a couple. Ask, "Are we connected?" If you're not, refer back to any of the above Love Links and get connected! This is a great opening for discussing anything that may have been neglected up until now. If you determine that your connection is thriving, honor your relationship and congratulate one another for the good work you are doing together.

LOVE LINK 10

BE A SOFT PLACE
TO FALL

Your bond with one another will deepen the more you are able to check in with one another and tell the truth about what you are experiencing. Trust builds, knowing that you can confide your ego struggles with your partner and not be judged or ill regarded. Because you have agreed to be in relationship with each other as the Spirits you are, the receiving of your truth telling can be greeted with unconditional love and acceptance. You will begin to appreciate each other more and more and, in time, you will become for each other what has been called "a soft place to fall."

To be your partner's soft place is a sacred act of trust. It means that you can come to that person with any issue or feeling. It means that no matter what, you are fully present to each other. You are both open to all that will be revealed and your love does not dwindle because of this deep sharing. To have this at the core of your relationship may be the greatest and most healing gift of all.

Make sure that in the busyness of your days you take time to be each other's soft place. Create opportunities to be available to one another. In a world that continues to challenge us emotionally in so many ways, it is crucial that we stay open and attentive to each other as much as possible.

Even as Love ascends to your height and caresses your tenderest branches that quiver in the sun,
So shall Love descend to your roots and shake them in their clinging to the earth.

KAHLIL GIBRAN

Practice compassion and someday you will be it.

JOAN CHITTISTER, OSB

CHAPTER 6

WEATHERING RELATIONSHIP STORMS: EGO BUSTERS

Even the most loving Soul Sailing couple will experience ego difficulties in the course of their relationship. As long as we are in human bodies with an Ego Broadcast Network trying to make itself heard, stormy seas will come our way. "Ego Busters" are techniques you can use as a couple to circumvent relationship storms or lessen their intensity.

You can also weather relationship storms together by keeping a keen perspective on them and remembering they do not have to affect who you are to one another. A storm is nothing more than two egos exchanging energy. It has nothing to do with the love you feel for one another as your Spirit selves. Hold a vision of your connection at all times. It can overcome any tendency to believe that your relationship is failing.

Like a storm at sea, wind gusts and huge swells form, but what is happening affects the surface waters only. Despite all the commotion, the ocean bed is intact and the creatures down below are just fine. When the storm stops, has anything really changed except at the surface? As in your relationship, the ocean floor, the Foundation, does not have to be affected by difficult times. The connection and Love are still there, completely undamaged because of who you are together, your Spirit selves. Keep your minds and hearts focused in this direction.

Trust that, in time, your relationship will come back to a place of equilibrium. Trust that you are being given a unique opportunity to learn important lessons that strengthen your Foundation, not weaken it. The storm is temporary and you will both learn and grow from it.

EGO BUSTER 1

SET POWERFUL INTENTIONS

There is nothing more influential when things are falling apart than the intentions you choose to hold. Your ability to stick to your intentions will determine the intensity and duration of any storms you might experience and how quickly you can come back together. Discuss what your intentions are for ego eruptions. Here are some powerful suggestions of intentions you may want to consider. They work very well with the Ego Busters presented in this section of the Toolbox.

Intentions

≫ To not wage battle with one another, but to help each other toward clarity.

≫ To see each other as true partners, not adversaries or enemies to be conquered.

→ To continue to move toward operating as your Spirit selves, no matter how difficult it may seem.

→ To use any and all tools available to prevent miscommunications from escalating.

Because storms are inevitable, try not to berate yourselves, assess blame, or harbor feelings of failure about having experienced a storm. Acknowledge that storms will come on occasion and commit to learn from each one as fully as you can. Remember that it takes skill and practice to become experienced sailors aboard any vessel, whether on the high seas or in the middle of your living room. Be compassionate with yourself and your partner, and acknowledge that you are engaged in the most challenging, yet rewarding, voyage of a lifetime.

EGO BUSTER 2

KEEP IT LIGHTHEARTED

Dealing with the ego doesn't always have to be a serious matter. If you can foster a lighthearted approach to your ego and its mechanisms, your relationship can remain fun and joy-filled. It is the ego operating system itself that tells you that relationships are difficult and very hard work. They are only hard work when you forget who you are to one another or don't use your tools.

Develop an "oh, well" attitude toward your ego and its messages. When it acts up, relax and reassure yourself that it is just doing what it does best: getting you upset. Being an ego scientist can be amusing and enlightening. The more you uncover its operating system, the freer you will be to have a lighter relationship with it and with your partner.

Bring humor into dealing with your Ego Broadcast episodes whenever possible. Remember the "Alien Abduction" we spoke about in Chapter 3? As a couple, you can do the same: create nicknames for certain patterns that the two of you fall into. Or create caricatures for specific parts of your ego selves. How about "Vince the Victim" or "Controlling Connie?" Imagine what your ego might look like if you were to draw a cartoon version of it. Could it look like a Neanderthal with a big club ready to clobber you over the head, a Darth Vader-like character stealthily planning your demise, or a nasty green gnome jumping up and down trying to get its way? These are three caricatures we've used that work for us. To say, "The Neanderthal is back!" reminds us that we can be playful, even when the ego comes to call.

Granted, sometimes in the middle of an intense storm humor might not be the best tool to use, but we can maintain a sense of lightheartedness about storms in general. Recognize that they will happen, so lighten up. When they do blow in, you don't have to give up the ship. After the winds die down, you may just find that an ego really is something to joke about!

EGO BUSTER 3

CHECK THE WEATHER REPORT

If you're feeling a storm brewing, stop what you're doing and check your internal weather report. Revisit your "feelings barometer" to determine where your vibration is. Ask yourself, "What is the strongest emotion within me right now? What is the Ego Broadcast saying?"

Consider taking a few minutes to write down your answers in a journal. This will help you move back into observer mode and separate yourself from the ego's energy. Journaling can bring clarity on an issue or pattern that keeps repeating itself. It can help you uncover unresolved issues that the ego will try to use to manipulate you again and again.

Many people say they literally feel better after writing. The very act of writing itself, putting pen to paper, is a physical way to release unwanted energy, to let go of any feelings keeping you in a low-vibration holding pattern. You may want to consider sharing your journal with your partner so you can both learn from the experience and move into a higher vibration together.

Is journaling not your cup of tea? Then do something different. Shift your attention elsewhere and onto other things. If you keep doing what you're doing, you will allow that agitated energy to build. Select a high vibration activity that energizes you in a positive way. Listen to music, exercise, go for a walk, read a book, call a friend, get out in nature, etc.—anything to move away from low-vibration thinking and feeling. This energy is experienced as much in our bodies as in our thoughts, so a physical release of it may be just what is needed. Change the scenery. Get up and move!

EGO BUSTER 4

CALL AN EGO AN EGO

As a storm brews, it is wise to remember that the person standing in front of you is your Beloved. Stay grounded in who you are to one another. Love, even in challenging times. When a situation escalates and emotions are running high for your partner, observe that he or she is simply caught in ego and is acting it out. The person you love didn't disappear, but an Ego Abduction has occurred. When someone says hurtful things, for example, it is helpful to recall that one's true essence is not saying those things. It is the human ego self that has taken over. The Spirit self is just out of reach, at least for the moment.

At times like these, set a strong intention for clarity. In the early stages of a disagreement, before escalation, it is actually possible to regain your footing and not be swept away by the ego. It is feasible that you can say to one another, "Wow, we are really acting out our egos right now, aren't we?" Moments of lucidity are available to see things as they really are. Wouldn't it be nice to look at each other, laugh, and say, "Well that was pretty nuts, wasn't it? We sure got grabbed by our egos, didn't we?" Stopping what you're doing, noticing what's happening, and calling an ego an ego can prevent the situation from worsening.

EGO BUSTER 5

THE LONE RANGER

Sometimes when your partner is headed for an Ego Abduction, it is possible to cut it off at the pass. Just like the Lone Ranger, you may have to step forward to lead the way and help your partner see what's happening. Like the television hero he was, the Lone Ranger was the one in the least fear, so he set out to circumvent serious situations. If you determine that you are the partner in the least fear (least caught up in the ego), it may be up to you to lead the way.

To keep an Ego Abduction from escalating, you can make some suggestions to your partner. You might say, "Is this really what we want, to go down this road? Do we really want to experience this?" A compassionate question, especially one with the word "we" is best, as it is not confrontational. The "we" is also more supportive and can subtly remind your loved one that you are indeed partners, not adversaries. (Use the word "I" and note how defensive the ego gets.) As the Lone Ranger, you can remind him or her how bad both of you are going to feel when the ego takes over. "This is going to hurt us. This is going to set us back."

Encourage your partner to focus on what messages the ego is broadcasting and to step back into observer mode. Move into speaking Spirit. "Tell me what your ego is saying," may be just the phrase to help take the blinders off and show in what direction your partner is headed.

Remember, the ego is a powerful abductor. The Lone Ranger can make an offering, but that doesn't ensure that the abductee will respond as hoped. It is worth a try. Just do the best you can in the moment. One of the best things you can do is to not join in. The ego loves an adversary, so choose other Ego Busters listed here and avoid stirring up the seas even more than they already are.

EGO BUSTER 6

MUTE THE MESSAGE

Often the best thing you can do when your partner has been abducted by ego is to be silent. Avoid trying to convince the abductee of the reality of the situation. It's amazing how, even with the strongest of intentions, one person's powerful ego can play upon another's and draw that person into the drama. In fact, that is exactly what energizes any ego encounter. An ego thrives on input, conversation, attempted reasoning—anything—so it can continue doing what it likes to do, engage and abduct.

It's a good idea to agree earlier that any time one of you is engaged with your ego, it's alright for the other person to remain silent, to not engage with their ego. Silence, in this case, is not about shutting down or distancing oneself. It's about collecting yourself and retaining your center for the good of the partnership. It's about buying valuable time to refocus on your Foundation and the Truth of who you are together, especially if your partner can't.

THE PAUSE THAT REFRESHES

Taking a time-out when things begin to escalate between the two of you is a very wise move. The time-out we refer to here is different than the one often used as a parenting strategy (usually as a form of punishment). This time-out can be as short as a few minutes or as long as a few hours. It's time used to move away from any negative energy that is beginning to spiral out of control. It's time to create space for each of you to come back to your center.

In truth, the fewer words that are said during an ego encounter, the quicker it will blow over. If you can catch yourselves at the beginning of a storm, perhaps at the earliest signs of an escalation, and take a pause, each person can take the ensuing quiet moments to reconnect with any other helpful tools to prevent a blowup.

You can each take a walk, go for a drive, or get out in nature. Moving into a different physical space lets the negative energy lessen its hold upon you. Usually a change of pace or scenery has that positive effect. Give each other some time and space to become the observer again, to relax and get centered.

Take a breather, literally. Breathing exercises can calm you and bring you back to your center. Try this one: breathe in your Foundation and remember who you are to one another. Take long, slow, deep inhalations and exhalations, the more the better. While you are breathing, focus on positive thoughts and feelings about your Foundation, how the We feels, how the two of you felt as original lovers. Remember who you are as Spirit and that your partner is your Beloved for many special reasons.

Time, in this case, is actually your ally. The pause that refreshes is not to escape the situation or to run away from one another. It is an intentional act that holds this time apart as good for you and necessary, so you can connect with your Spirit selves.

EGO BUSTER 8

SMOOTH SOME FEATHERS

We often forget how powerful human touch can be to shift negative energy into positive energy. Granted, when in the midst of an ego abduction, some people truly don't want to be touched. For most people though, that is exactly what they need when the ego comes to call. While it may seem that the ego self is looking for a fight, the person is actually looking for love and affection.

Imagine your partner as the Spirit self he or she truly is, angelic in nature. Remember, angels can have some pretty ruffled feathers. Smooth down those bristled feathers with gentle strokes, a hug, or hand holding. Sit close together, shoulder-to-shoulder. Lie down together (review Love Link 4). Make loving eye contact. Open yourselves to one another in this way instead of shutting down and you may be surprised how quickly that wily ego slinks away.

Discuss ahead of time what displays of affection each of you might be most receptive to at times like these and set the intention to use them. Your physical connection can break the spell of any spiraling negative energy. One technique that is especially effective in staying open and receptive to one another is to place your flat palm on your partner's heart center (4th Chakra), mid-chest, front and/or back. Connecting with the heart center in this way can dissolve negative energy and emotions. It's also an intimate and loving act that brings the two of you closer together. Don't discount the power of touch to help you make the shift from ego to Spirit.

EGO BUSTER 9

HOLD A SPACE

Sometimes when an ego abduction has occurred, there really is nothing you can do or say that will bring your partner back to a higher state of consciousness. This is another of the Lone Ranger's roles: to remain in a state of love and compassion for the other. It's called "holding a space." This is a state of thought and feeling that acknowledges that your loved one is struggling and is in emotional difficulty. An intention grows inside of you to see your partner returning soon to the loving arms of your relationship. You may even speak this intention aloud. "I am going to wait for you to come back. I love you and I can't wait for us to be connected again."

As the one in the least fear, again, you may be asked to take the lead in your relationship, but this time it is not with words, but through your ability to stay centered and hold your partner in a heart embrace. You may want to meditate and actually envision them letting go of their angst and opening to love. Visualize them coming to peace, their heart opening and remembering love, receiving love. You may want to pray for them.

From the very Foundation of your relationship, from the We that you are together, send such loving thoughts as: "I am sorry you are having a hard time right now. I am holding you in compassion." Though the ego may attempt to block this message, your Beloved's consciousness may feel your unconditional loyalty as the Beloved partner who is patiently waiting out the storm.

Operating in this way is a very high-vibration state, and you will continue to feel its benefits after you come back together. When your loved one "returns," you will be in a good space yourself because you have not been upset or angry. You have remained in compassion for them, and your "coming back together time" will be optimized. Remember, a single ego storm is much easier to deal with than a dual ego storm.

EGO BUSTER 10

ASK FOR HELP

You are surrounded by Divine assistance at all times. When you're in the midst of a storm, it's an excellent time to ask those angelic helpers to show up and give you a hand. Because you have free will, your helpers will not force their way into any situation, so it is up to you to ask for guidance or support to shift a negative encounter.

Asking for help is actually an act of raising your vibration because your thoughts are on something of a higher nature. Acknowledging the presence and availability of that energy can connect you with your Spirit self in surprising ways. You may feel an immediate sense of calm wash over you. That is a clue that your vibration is shifting. You may receive insights into things you can say or do to tap back into the Love between you and your partner. You may find yourself moving into observer mode, gaining insight into the situation and even remembering tools from the Toolbox that could be helpful.

The God-energy that you are a part of is always present and available. It is only your ego self that convinces you it is far away or unresponsive. It may seem distant to you because of how badly you are feeling in the moment. Your petition for assistance allows you to automatically tap into that ongoing connection of Love, which is really only a thought away.

I am like a falling star who has finally found her place next to another in a lovely constellation, where we will sparkle in the heavens forever.

AMY TAN

At times our own light goes out and is rekindled by a spark from another person. Each of us has cause to think with deep gratitude of those who have lighted the flame within us.

ALBERT SCHWEITZER

CHAPTER 7

COASTING BACK INTO LOVE: HEART MENDERS

It takes time for any of us to come back into the arms of Love after we have experienced either our own or our partner's Ego Abduction. The "Heart Menders" presented here can help you come back together. Allow yourselves plenty of time and space to do so. Each person will recover from the ego's bruising effects at his or her own pace. Compassion is in order here. We cannot expect that we will feel deep connectedness for one another right away, especially in the aftermath of a full-blown storm. The ego has worked very hard to separate us, immersing us in strong, divisive emotions.

When it feels right, you can begin to live out the intentions you set earlier and begin the process of coming back together. It is key to your growth as individuals and as a couple that you set aside adequate time to reconnect so you can explore what you can learn from this episode. Just as in sailing, when your vessel becomes battered from a brief scrape on an unforeseen reef, or fairly disabled from being dashed upon a rocky shore, you can regroup, rebuild, examine what happened, and learn from your mistakes. With camaraderie and teamwork, you will set sail once again, stronger than ever, clearly focused on living in Perfect Love.

HEART MENDER 1

REMEMBER THE LOVE, AGAIN

Acknowledge your desire to come back together and move into connection slowly. Be gentle with one another. Take baby steps to remember who you are together, one another's Beloved. Review the Love Links in Chapter 5 and select one or more to focus on. Getting out in nature or meditating together can be especially helpful. Any of the Links described there will assist you in raising your vibration and coming back together as your Spirit selves.

Activities that nurture with minimal conversation are key during the early stages of reconnecting. To launch into dialogue about what happened may be premature and give the ego another opportunity to make itself heard. While quiet, you can listen deeply to your own inner workings and notice how your ego may still be lurking around. Foster a sense of positive and nurturing stillness between the two of you, one that will help you remember the Love.

Re-establish your physical connection as soon as possible. Look into each other's eyes. Hug. Stroke. Touch. Close the physical distance between you that the ego has tried to create. Allow your bodies to bring you home to one another.

HEART MENDER 2

TELL THE TRUTH

When the time feels right, you may want to tell a few simple truths about what happened. Simply acknowledge that you were grabbed by your separate egos; that you went through a bad time and that you really do want to reconnect. Speak aloud your desire to merge and be the couple you were before things began to fall apart. If you have missed each other, say so. Notice how your heart naturally wants to open up to your partner when language like this is spoken. When you speak the truth of your desire to be Beloveds to one another, you intensify the power of your intention to come back together, and you will naturally begin to move in that direction.

Listen to your partner with your heart, not your head. You may want to actually envision your heart opening to receive all that is being shared. It is as if you are using a new sort of hearing device in the middle of your chest. Keep your attention placed there as your sharing time begins, and notice how you are able to listen differently. You are now in a place of centeredness instead of one of busy mind chatter, listening with compassion instead of judgment.

HEART MENDER 3

BE EGO SCIENTISTS

Begin a dialogue to identify what happened. This first "coming back together time" to talk will only be fruitful if both parties speak about their own process. Each of you will need to take responsibility for how your ego operated. Begin by using Spirit talk as we outlined in Chapter 5. Use third-person language about what the ego broadcast said, how it affected you, and the choices you made as a result of it. Speaking in this way, you become the scientist, taking a more dispassionate stance about all that happened. Doing so does not lessen the importance of the incident. It simply keeps the ego at bay and allows the two of you to connect on a higher level.

As you begin dialogue, continue to be aware of how your ego may still be trying to lure you in: finding fault with your partner, blaming, listing all of your hurts, etc. It does no good to speak in this way, as it opens a door for the ego broadcast to be heard all over again. If it does (and in many cases it will), this means that you're still hooked; the broadcast is still sending messages, desiring that you be *right* and making your partner *wrong* for what happened. In this case, more time for centering may be required before you can truly come back together. If more time and space is needed for each of you to return to center and operate as your Spirit selves, take that time and space.

Imagine yourself at this point in the coming-back-together process as "ego detectives." Together, shine a beam on all the ego's shadowy places and lay everything you notice about how your ego self operates out on a table. Look at it all carefully, dispassionately. Remember that what is illuminated can never affect you in the same way again. This process loosens the ego's grip on you, especially in terms of future storms. When you can identify how your ego likes to operate, you can learn to interrupt its broadcast before it gets too loud and wreaks havoc on your relationship. Dissecting an ego in this way, after a storm, can truly disempower it.

There is also a deepening factor at work here, for when you know what each other's abductors are, you develop greater compassion for one another. You've witnessed firsthand how easily each of you can be abducted and you sympathize, understanding how hard it can be to turn away from the ego broadcast and resist its call. Your bond strengthens when you can be ego scientists together. It is one more step in acknowledging who you really are, spirits having a human experience together!

HEART MENDER 4

SPEAK YOUR LEARNING

After satisfactorily illuminating how your ego selves chose to operate, talk about what each of you learned as a result. What insights did you gain as individuals?

The landscape of your relationship will shift once again when you hear your partner speak about his or her ego and what was learned from this experience. This is a very powerful and sacred time together, bearing witness to another's illumination. You may even feel energized by this part of the process, feeling your vibration rise because you can literally feel yourself and your partner growing in awareness. You will also begin to feel a deeper level of intimacy because you have not only survived a storm together, but are thriving as a result. You have grown through a tempest, and that is a powerful act.

After speaking about what you learned, you will recognize that you have a myriad of choices of how to do things differently next time. You also understand that you don't have to repeat this same lesson with the proper choices. It is comforting to know that as true Spirit partners, your Foundation is strong enough to weather any storms that might head your way.

HEART MENDER 5

SAY IT WITH LETTERS

If you are having a hard time communicating verbally, try connecting through journal writing. A couple's journal can be very helpful in opening up communication after a storm. You are now listening from a different perspective!

Leave a blank book (journal) open on a table. Whenever you are so guided, write a note to one another, sharing your thoughts on any number of things: how your ego broadcast may have affected you, what you learned, or the current state of your vibration. Journaling in such a way can also reveal whether you are still speaking through your ego, especially if you find yourself tempted to vent on paper about the storm and what you went through, or to point a finger of blame at your partner.

Your partner can respond to you in writing and share his or her experience, or respond positively to yours. Remember, as Beloveds you are here to support one another, and your mutual goal is to come back together as soon as possible. Express your Love in small notes to one another. Express any sense of regret you might feel. Apologize if you need to. By telling the truth and being openhearted, you'll find yourselves longing to experience your Perfect Love again.

HEART MENDER 6

LIVE YOUR INTENTIONS

Take time to determine what went wrong in your communication to create such a storm, and set the intention to do things differently next time. This may be the most important phase of your coming-back-together time because you have the unique opportunity to make a pact together to change the course of your relationship.

There are always things you'll wish hadn't been said or done during a storm. Look at those and identify your patterns. Did you attack? Name call? Shut down? Every ego has its own way of taking control, so what mechanisms did yours use? Notice what it is you personally bring in to each argument. Your ego will try to use this tactic again and again until you shine a light on it and disempower it.

Discuss what each of you could have done differently. Assess how well you used the tools available to you in the Toolbox. Did your egos convince you not to use them, or did you just plain forget because of the swiftness of the abduction? Together create a new game plan for next time. Perhaps try a different Ego Buster from the Toolbox. There is no specific way to respond to storms, so initially you may have to experiment to find what works best for you. Trust that you will find your own unique solutions, and that guidance is available to help you do so.

Set new intentions for how the two of you will respond to relationship storms in the future. Vow to be more present to one another as your Spirit selves. Remember that you are partners in growth, and that growth is limitless, so there will always be more valuable lessons to learn together.

HEART MENDER 7

FORGIVE AND LET GO

If at the end of your coming-back-together time you are still experiencing twinges of hurt or blame, let go of any hurt feelings that may be hanging onto the edges of your heart and relinquish them. It is time to forgive. Otherwise, those feelings that are still rooted in the ego will keep you separated from one another.

Forgiveness is about freedom. *Freeing yourself* from any final efforts on the ego's part to stay in charge will release you from feeling upset. Forgiveness is about moving out of low-vibration thinking and feeling, and back into a higher-vibrational range. Forgiveness is about letting go of anything that holds you back from feeling absolutely wonderful and being your Spirit self.

After an Ego Abduction you may have to forgive yourself for falling prey to your ego once again. Tap into the vibration of compassion, and let go of any sense of guilt. Forgive your partner for succumbing to the influence of ego, as well. Forgiveness is not so much about forgetting, but about remembering who you truly are to one another: Love, unconditional Love, Love without the ego. Surrender what remains of the ego and dive back into the waters of Love.

HEART MENDER 8

GROW IN GRATITUDE

Gratitude carries one of the highest vibrations we can access. You will notice that anytime you are feeling particularly grateful for something or someone in your life, a profound sense of well-being will ripple through your body/mind. Even after a storm, you can tap into the vibration of gratitude for having experienced it because it has brought you to new shores of awareness.

Acknowledge and affirm your newfound insights—both yours and your partner's. Offer a prayer of gratitude for the lessons that have come, and your ability to grow anew from this experience. Offer gratitude for the deepened intimacy you now feel as a result of the storm you've just weathered. See the perfection in all of it for having brought you closer together than ever before. Then, offer gratitude for one another as Divine traveling companions and celebrate your journey home to Perfect Love together.

THE PERFECT LOVE TOOLBOX
QUICK REFERENCE GUIDE

Smooth Sailing — Love Links

1. Speak Spirit
2. Remember the Love
3. Sit Higher Up in the Bleachers
4. Loving Touch
5. Show and Tell
6. Meditate Together
7. Do What You Love
8. Create Sacred Space
9. Check In with Each Other
10. Be a Soft Place to Fall

Weathering Relationship Storms — Ego Busters

1. Set Powerful Intentions
2. Keep It Lighthearted
3. Check the Weather Report
4. Call an Ego an Ego
5. The Lone Ranger
6. Mute the Message
7. The Pause that Refreshes
8. Smooth Some Feathers
9. Hold a Space
10. Ask for Help

Coasting Back into Love—Heart Menders

1. Remember the Love, Again
2. Tell the Truth
3. Be Ego Scientists
4. Speak Your Learning
5. Say It with Letters
6. Live Your Intentions
7. Forgive and Let Go
8. Grow in Gratitude

Part III

The Shores of
Perfect Love

*We are the leaves of one branch, the drops of one sea,
the flowers of one garden.*

JEAN BAPTISTE HENRY LACORDAIRE

*Love is a fleeting moment unless you reach
a different stage of love,
where love is no more a relationship
but a state of being.*

OSHO

CHAPTER 8

SCANNING THE HORIZON: A NEW WORLD AWAITS

We began this journey to Perfect Love by asking you to imagine. Imagine what your life might be like if unconditional love was yours. What it might feel like to know you've been partnered with a very special person with whom you will journey to your most sacred self. Imagine together, you'll do just that.

As this book draws to an end, we invite you to return once more to the canvas of your imagination. Now, consider how different your life might be, this time on a very practical level, if you applied the Soul Sailing principles we've shared here. Just imagine…

… a serene, yet joyous, partnership with much less drama, and fewer emotional highs and lows. Your energy level remains high because you choose not to climb aboard the energy-sapping roller coaster of ego-based emotions. A subtle sense of clarity and balance now flows through your days.

… arguments as a thing of the past. Because you are learning to ignore the ego's messages and the conflicts they create, you experience an enhanced sense of companionship with your partner. You desire to be each other's best friend, spending more and more quality time

together. You enjoy nurturing each other. Your passion is high, your intimacy deep.

... personal and relationship freedom. You've learned that you can actually choose which "self" you would like to experience, your ego or your Spirit self. This choice is made moment by moment in every encounter. The ability to choose brings a new sense of freedom, and with freedom comes opportunity. As a Soul Sailor, you have the opportunity to transform yourself and your relationship into whatever you wish them to be. You have control, you have the power. You can create the life of your heart's desires, based on Divine never-ending Love.

... a greater sense of inner peace. By turning away from the ego's broadcasts, your mind has become less distracted by extraneous noise. Inner calm now prevails. Without having to deal with the ego's distracting chatter, your mind is open to new empowering thoughts and perceptions. Clarity is easily accessed, focus is heightened, creativity flows.

... enhanced health and emotional well-being. By monitoring your vibration, you now have the ability to determine how good or bad you feel. When you choose higher thoughts and emotions in the Spirit range, you feel better whenever you wish. Your stress level will lower, persistent ailments may disappear, and you'll find yourself feeling healthier than ever before. You will also enjoy greater longevity and freedom from dis-ease, because your body is no longer subjected to the detrimental effects of an energy-sapping ego.

... dramatic lifestyle changes. When you set the intention to maintain a high vibration, every area of your life will be enhanced. You will notice a strong ambition to live in alignment with your Spirit's calling. You will want to regularly engage in high-vibration activities. You may find yourself spending more time in nature, eating fresh foods, getting more exercise, surrounding yourself with beauty, seeking solitude, or simply appreciating silence. All of these things are indicative of a new you, one who honors the Spirit within.

As the days and weeks of your new life unfold, you will continue to stay connected to your Spirit self, as well as to your partner's Spirit self. You will also fine-tune your ability to notice the ego's workings and choose not to respond to them. You will make consistent positive choices that allow you to spend more and more time each day as your Spirit self. When you do, you'll discover that the benefits we have described here have multiplied a hundredfold, manifesting in ways you never dreamed possible.

And then one day, perhaps upon waking, you'll look about you and realize how different your world seems, how much you have grown, how much Love and joy enrich your life. Congratulations! You have come home to your Spirit self. You are now fully able to express your truest identity, Perfect Love, to the rest of the world!

Despite all of the remarkable changes that have occurred in your life thus far, there are more to come. The journey is far from over. In fact, the next leg, the most profound and far-reaching segment of your voyage to Perfect Love is about to begin.

A Divine Directive

When you can live in the world on a more continuous basis as your Spirit self, you will begin to feel an excitement growing within you to share your Perfect Love with others. Love, as you know, cannot be contained. It does not belong to any one individual or even one perfectly loving partnership. It naturally wants to pour out onto others. So, don't be surprised when the subtle inclination you are feeling to "spread the Love" turns into a full-force gale—a divinely sourced directive to Soul Sail with everyone you meet.

It is time for you to do just that, to take everything you've learned about Perfect Love and apply it to every single relationship in your life. This is a natural process that requires no additional techniques other than those we have already shown you. This is because there are no differences between the Perfect Love you experience with your Beloved and the Perfect Love you can experience with anyone who comes into your life. Whether they be intimate relationships or casual, you can apply the same principles. Each person is simply another version of your Beloved. Your divine calling is to embrace each man, woman, and child as his or her Spirit self—just as you would your intimate partner.

This is your ultimate destiny, the highest purpose to which you have been called—to be a natural purveyor of Divine Love and compassion. Your personal experience of unconditional love has been nurtured, until now, through your intimate relationship. Rest assured, even at this point in your journey, if you don't have a partner, you can still experience Perfect Love on your own with anyone you choose, for YOU are the source of that Perfect Love, not another person. YOU have the capability to express your Spirit self, the embodiment of Perfect Love, to everyone you meet.

Your next step, therefore, is to expand the Perfect Love found within you and let it loose in the world. Relate to everyone who crosses your path, spirit-to-spirit, as brothers and sisters sourced in one Universal Spirit. This is the great work we have been created for, and, yet, it is not work at all, only a natural outpouring of who we really are to one another—Love.

Become a Purveyor of Love

By being your Spirit self with others, you will now set into motion a series of events that will change your world as you know it. It will also dramatically shift the inner world of each person with whom you come in contact. You will notice this happening in three different ways:

First, you will observe people being drawn to you, even without benefit of conversation. They may watch you intently. They may express a desire to be close to you, to spend time with you. It may feel as if you are a beacon of some sort, and by doing nothing more than being your love-filled self, you attract others with your brightness. Like a magnet, you will draw others toward you because you naturally emanate the high-vibration qualities of hospitality, openheartedness, understanding, and acceptance. They will desire to connect with you because you outpour what they would like to feel within themselves—more happiness, personal peace, and love. Instead of challenging their ego, your presence calms them, inviting them, on a very subtle level, to feel how different life could be.

If you recall, in the Introduction to this book, we assured you that if you did not currently have a partner to experience Perfect Love with, that was quite alright. In fact, upon reading and practicing the techniques outlined here, don't be surprised if a new partner comes into your life. That's because the phenomenon we have just described, personal magnetism, invites potential partners in to meet you. Your high vibration makes you irresistible to others when you are able to relate to them through your Spirit self. Imagine your possibilities!

Second, by being your Spirit self, you offer others a great opportunity. You give them permission to be their Spirit selves too! By the simple act of operating as Spirit, you invite them, by your perfectly loving presence, to explore what it might be like for them to live and love in a similar way.

Third, when you can hold a consistent vibration of peace and love, then connect with another through your very presence, you may facilitate a monumental opening of their own heart center. Such an occurrence is not uncommon. You may have heard that a dramatic shift in awareness can happen in the presence of an enlightened other. As a purveyor of Perfect Love, you, too, can serve as a gateway to personal freedom for someone else. Your loving energy can literally open their blocked or closed heart. Your light-filled presence can reacquaint them with their own.

Ripples and More Ripples

This is the ultimate act of service you are here to perform: to live so fully, so vibrantly as your Spirit self, that by your very presence, you embody the Love of Spirit, of God—and lives are transformed because of it. We are all here to be Love to one another.

By embracing yourself as Spirit, you become a swell in a glorious sea of Divine Love. When you ripple out to others in love, you welcome them home to their Spirit selves, and the love expands. You enable them to reach out to others in the same way, and before you know it, you have not only created ripples of love, but waves of love that can transform and heal all of your relationships.

Imagine what life could be like if this love continued to expand, if it moved through our families, out into our neighborhoods and towns. Imagine waves of love continuing to roll, building in intensity, surging across boundaries and borders into other countries, dissolving barriers between people and nations. This Sea of Love grows in scope, in power, until everything in its path is absorbed by it, enlivened and healed by it. Until everything, everyone, is awash in Love. What will our world be like if Love is all there is?

To Dwell in Possibility

If we are to usher in a world of Perfect Love, as many of us as possible are needed. By standing steady as your Divine self, connecting with others spirit-to-spirit, you will join the great armada which has already set sail to establish a global experience of Perfect Love. YOU can play a key role in creating the world we have all been dreaming of, one characterized by peace, love, and freedom for all.

In his life-changing book, *The Last Hours of Ancient Sunlight*, author Thom Hartmann confirms that a planetary shift such as this, one united in love, is truly possible. It is simply a matter of arithmetic. He explains a theory that states that a mere 80,000 people are needed to create a shift in consciousness.* What that means to us is 80,000 people oriented toward Love will be enough to transform our reality. It also means that an experience of Perfect Love is a real possibility for every single person who walks this planet. And that is an exciting notion, indeed!

"Is such a world really possible?" you might ask. Perhaps the new world we propose here, the world of Perfect Love, feels too simplistic to you, or impossible to create. We wouldn't be surprised if those exact thoughts were dancing through your mind right now. Those are ego-based thoughts, remember? As we've discussed, the ego is rooted in fear, doubt, pessimism, and the like, emotions that sap our positive energy and keep us separated from our highest selves. Consider this, if a new world is a genuine possibility, one rooted in Love, wouldn't it be "normal" for the ego to try and disperse that energy? Of course! The ego will do everything in its power to keep us separated from one another.

This is the primary reason why we have consistently failed to create a world embodying Perfect Love. It is because the ego is sourced in feelings of inferiority and fear, which we make manifest

---

* "... *according to the laws of wave mechanics ... two waves added together are four times as intense as one wave, ten waves are one hundred times as intense, etc. Since thought is energy, and all energy occurs in waves ... 80,000 people all thinking the same thing together are as powerful, in terms of creating the reality that we all share as the 6,400,000,000 people (80,000 times 80,000) on the planet ...*"

in our actions. If we believe we are different from one another, or superior, if we perceive other people to be flawed or wrong, we'll disconnect from them, and perfectly loving relationships will be impossible to create.

Coming Home to Love

Knowing this, how do we finally move beyond the ego's influence to usher in a global experience of Perfect Love? We join hands, link our hearts and set sail—*together*. We become loyal traveling companions by forming our own support system, a community of Perfect Love-ers, and unifying our efforts to live and love as our Spirit selves.

Let us take the first steps in recognizing and celebrating our Oneness. It is through our eternal interconnectedness that we will unleash the inspiration, the strength, and the courage needed to stay the course, ultimately making manifest the global experience of Perfect Love we seek.

May we embrace one another and live as One, for when we do, we will come home to the Love we have all been longing for...

A BLESSING FOR LOVE

What a powerful journey we have begun together! We are grateful you have chosen to spend this time with us within these pages. We are honored you have answered the call to join us, along with thousands of others like yourself, and taken the first steps toward creating the world we long for, a world of peace, equity, and Love for all.

As this particular passage of our voyage comes to an end, we'd like to leave you with a special benediction, penned with love, from our hearts to yours. We call it "A Blessing for Love." May it sustain you in the days and weeks ahead as your own journey to Perfect Love unfolds...

A BLESSING FOR LOVE

As you rise up in the morning with a smile in your heart
May you feel the warmth of the sun on your face
And smell the beauty of the season in the air

May gratitude fill your being
For health of body and mind
And for food that nourishes you and keeps you strong

Gratitude for the presence of animals and pets
Who give love without conditions
Who wait, depend, and serve so loyally

May appreciation of family and friends course through your veins
Thanking them for love well given
For good times and bad
For helping you grow into who you are today

May your heart be filled with tenderness
As you gaze upon the wizened faces of the elderly
Grateful for their hard work and leadership

May your Spirit run and dance and play with the children
As they soar across the playground
Free from cares or worries, moment-led creatures

May you remember the possibilities of Love
When you witness a seasoned,

married couple devotedly gazing into each other's eyes
Gently caressing hands and spirits

May you see the uniqueness of each human being who crosses your path today
Letting go of all judgments or opinions that keep you separate from them
Sending them a secret blessing as you pass on the street
"I honor you, my friend, for simply being who you are."

For those who suffer and struggle through their days
May your heart be rooted in compassion to transform their suffering
May you experience them as Children of God with hopes and dreams

May you be respectful of all who live and worship differently than you do
May you see them through angel eyes
Beings of beauty and brilliance
Your brothers and sisters

May you remember daily who you are and who you can become
Of all that is available to you as a Child of the Universe
How Love can be the cloak you wear
Peace be the shoes with which you walk upon the Earth

May you remember this day to mirror the Divine
And be peace and Love to all...

Perfect Love,
Brad and Jan Lundy
March 2006

ACKNOWLEDGMENTS

We begin this litany of blessings by thanking Spirit for bringing us together so we could experience the most powerful Love of all, Perfect Love.

Loving thanks to our mothers, Marilyn Lundy Mason and Lorraine Deremo, for their generous hearts and loving spirits. Your support means more to us than you will ever know.

Gratitude to our family and friends, who continue to love and support us as we journey deeper into our Spirit selves.

Appreciation to our mentors, friends in growth who read galleys, offered insights and kind words for this body of work. Because of you, the Love will spread more quickly.

Special thanks to our extraordinary production team, Mary Jo Zazueta (To The Point Solutions) and Mike Dudek (Dudek Design), for making this book the beautiful offering it is. We couldn't have done this without you.

Chocolate hugs and heartfelt thanks to Claire Gerus for encouragement, and for sharing your consulting and editing skills with us in such an openhearted and generous way. You are simply the best!

And, finally, a special tribute to two of our mentors who opened up a whole new world for each of us. For Brad, Richard Bach and *Jonathan Livingston Seagull*. For Jan, Wayne Dyer, and *The Awakened Life*. May Spirit continue to bless you!

REFERENCES

Hartmann, Thom. *The Last Hours of Ancient Sunlight: The Fate of the World and What We Can Do Before It's Too Late*. New York: Three Rivers Press, 2004.

Pert, Candace B., Ph.D. *The Molecules of Emotion: Why You Feel the Way You Feel*. New York, NY: Scribner, 1997.

RECOMMENDED READING

The following books and their authors were influential in our spiritual formation during our journey to *Perfect Love*. We highly recommend them to you.

Bach, Richard. *Illusions: The Adventures of a Reluctant Messiah*. Delacorte Press, 1977.

Dyer, Dr. Wayne W. *The Power of Intention: Change the Way You Look at Things and the Way You Look at Things Will Change*. Carlsbad, CA: Hay House, 2004.

Harvey, Andrew. *The Way of Passion: A Celebration of Rumi*. Berkeley, CA: Frog, Ltd., 1994.

Kingma, Daphne Rose. *Finding True Love: The 4 Essential Keys to Discovering the Love of Your Life*. Berkeley, CA: Conari Press, 1996.

Kingma, Daphne Rose. *The Future of Love: The Power of the Soul in Intimate Relationships.* New York, NY: Random House, 1998.

Kasl, Ph.D., Charlotte. *If the Buddha Dated: A Handbook for Finding Love on a Spiritual Path.* New York, NY: Penguin Putnam, 1999.

Loggins, Kenny and Julia. *The Unimaginable Life: Lessons Learned on the Path to Love.* New York, NY: Avon Books, 1997.

Martin, William. *The Couple's Tao Te Ching: A New Interpretation.* New York, NY: Marlowe and Co., 2000.

Thoele, Sue Patton. *Heart Centered Marriage: Fulfilling Our Natural Desire For Sacred Partnership.* Berkeley, CA: Conari Press, 1996.

Vanzant, Iyanla. *In the Meantime: Finding Yourself and the Love You Want.* New York, NY: Simon & Schuster, 1998.

Walsch, Neale Donald. *Conversations with God: An Uncommon Dialogue, (Book 1).* New York, NY: G. P. Putnam's Sons, 1996.

Waters, Owen. *The Shift: The Revolution in Human Consciousness.* Delaware, USA: Infinite Being Publishing, 2006.

GLOSSARY OF TERMS

Ego Abduction—*when an individual gets dramatically hooked in by the ego and expresses him or herself through it, especially in uncharacteristic ways.*

Ego Broadcast Network—*another term for the human ego system and the messages it sends.*

Ego Busters—*techniques you can use as a couple to circumvent relationship storms or lessen their intensity.*

Ego Identity—*another term for your ego self.*

Ego Operating System—*the mental/emotional system within you that is dominated by the ego; the blueprint for what it means to be a human being on a primitive level.*

Ego Self—*that aspect of your human self which is sourced in fear and the lower emotions; a false self.*

Heart Menders—*steps you can take as a couple to cruise back into Love after a relationship storm.*

Inner Compass—*a variety of tools to help you identify when you are operating as your Spirit self or through your ego self, including "Right Foot, Left Foot," "Checking in with Yourself," and "Assessing Your Love Quotient."*

Love Links—*personal practices you and your partner can use to keep your connection strong, enhancing the day-to-day quality of your relationship.*

Perfect Love—*what you will experience when you choose to love another as his or her Spirit self, instead of the human being you have perceived him or her to be.*

Perfect Love Network—*a virtual support community for people dedicated to living as their Spirit selves who seek a greater experience of Perfect Love. Found on the Web at www.soulsailing.com.*

Right Foot, Left Foot—*a technique to help you determine if you are operating as your Spirit self or as your ego self. Right foot represents Spirit; left foot represents ego.*

Soul Companion—*anyone with whom you are in a relationship for the ultimate purpose of soul growth.*

Speaking From Spirit—*expressing the (positive) thoughts and feelings that come from your spirit, sourced in love and compassion.*

Speaking Through Your Ego—*expressing the (negative) thoughts and feelings that come from your ego, predominately rooted in fear.*

Spirit—*God, the All, the Infinite Source of which we are a part, which flows through us and all around us.*

Spirit Identity—*another term for your Spirit self.*

Spirit Self—*who you are as your truest Divine self; the human embodiment of Love and compassion.*

Soul Sailing—*the method used to access Perfect Love by living in the world as your Spirit self.*

Vibration—*to what extent you are feeling the presence of your Spirit self and the positive qualities associated with it, including peace, joy, compassion, and love.*

Vibration of Love—*the highest level of vibration you can experience as your Spirit self, characterized by complete love for self and others.*

ABOUT THE AUTHORS

BRAD LUNDY is a publisher, author, and spiritual counselor. His entrepreneurial spirit has led him to create various businesses over the years, most rooted in his love of the earth and wellness. He enjoys mentoring others, especially in the area of magazine publishing. His was the vision behind the success of *Healing Garden Journal* which he founded in 2000.

In the mid '90s, Brad launched an energy-healing practice that enabled him to combine his passion for health and well-being with his desire to companion others as they awaken to their true identity—Spirit. Today his passion put into practice is called "Soul Sailing." Through all he does, Brad remains committed to creating a global community rooted in compassion, peace, and prosperity for all.

JANICE LYNNE LUNDY is a former educator, nationally recognized speaker, and the author of *Coming Home to Ourselves: A Woman's Journey to Wholeness* and *Awakening the Spirit Within*—highly acclaimed books that encourage us to live deeply authentic lives. Since 1998, Jan has penned a personal/spiritual growth column for *Women's Lifestyle*, a nationally syndicated, monthly magazine.

Her love of supporting other people as they journey through life is enhanced via her work as an Interfaith Spiritual Director. She also serves as adjunct staff for The Institute of Spirituality, Dominican Center at Marywood in Grand Rapids, MI, mentoring spiritual directors in training.

For five years, Brad and Jan Lundy were co-publishers of *Healing Garden Journal*, Michigan's premier wellness magazine, with a statewide circulation of over 125,000 readers. Today, they serve as its Consulting Editors and co-author a column on "Perfect Love."

Brad and Jan have been Soul Sailing together for five years now and feel blessed to be soul companions to one another. Between them, they have seven children and two grandchildren who keep them joyfully busy. They work, live, and play along the peaceful shores of the Grand Traverse Bay in Michigan.

PRIVATE SOUL SAILING
LESSONS WITH BRAD LUNDY

Brad Lundy has had a private Soul Sailing practice since 2000. He delights in assisting others open up to their Spirit selves.

*Imagine having a friend that honors you as the Divine Spirit
you truly are.
Someone who knows the answers to life and Love
reside within your heart.
Someone who guides you in living the joy that fills your soul.
A friend who leaves you feeling peaceful, whole, and connected.*

Soul Sailing is a journey with just such a friend and guide. Over the telephone, in a 30 to 60 minute conversation, Brad can support you in connecting to your Spirit self, so you can resolve personal difficulties, including relationship issues.

Visit www.soulsailing.com or call (800) 831-3230 to learn more, read what Soul Sailing clients have to say, and obtain consultation rates and availability times.

Perfect Love Group Presentations

Learn how your organization or network of friends can host a Perfect Love presentation with Brad and Jan Lundy in your community by visiting www.soulsailing.com.

THE PERFECT LOVE NETWORK: SUPPORT FOR YOUR JOURNEY

As a Soul Sailing couple, we've learned how important support can be as we journey to Perfect Love. The transition from ego-based to Spirit-filled living has its challenges. Both of us are so very grateful that we've had each other to lean on while learning to Soul Sail. As time has passed, Soul Sailing has become easier for us. But, because we are still walking this earth in two human bodies, we do occasionally stumble and fall, get abducted by our egos, and temporarily lose sight of the love we share. Thankfully, we have one another to reorient ourselves back toward Spirit. We know that you will need others to lean on, too, just as we have. In fact, in the early stages, we believe it best that you not attempt to journey beyond ego without the proper support.

When you first begin your voyage to Perfect Love, it's easy to fall prey to the ego's broadcasts. On some level, the ego knows that it's losing its power and influence over you, so it will most likely turn up its volume and transmit all sorts of demoralizing messages. "This is too hard," "You're not cut out for this work," or "Love isn't meant to be yours," may be some of the disempowering rhetoric it sends your way. Don't be surprised at anything your ego might say or do during this transition-to-Spirit time.

The Perfect Love Network can provide you with all the support you need for your journey to Love at www.soulsailing.com. Within this virtual community, you'll meet other caring individuals who desire to live as Spirit, just like you. You'll find answers to your important Soul Sailing questions and one-on-one support for any challenges you're facing. You may find the Community Forum to be especially helpful. This is where the authors and Soul Sailors at all levels of transition hang out. When your ego turns up the volume and overpowers you (Ego Abduction!), you can easily disregard all the progress you've made if there's no one to help you stay connected to your Spirit self. And, if your vibration is low, chatting with fellow Soul Sailors can help. It's also a great place to share your Soul Sailing/Perfect Love success stories.

At www.soulsailing.com, you'll be delighted to find other supportive resources as well, including articles, books, inspiring gifts for your Soul Sailing companions, a calendar of events, and a newsletter to keep you informed on all things Soul Sailing!

One thing you'll notice about the Perfect Love Network is that everyone comes as they are and contributes however they can for the good of the community. No matter where you are on your journey, from first launch to world traveler, there is a place for you here. If your desire is to read, watch, or listen, we honor that. If it's to contribute from your well of personal experience by actively posting, sharing tips, or submitting articles, we honor that as well.

If your soul has caught fire to share Soul Sailing with others, we invite you to participate on another level. It may feel important for you to physically get together with others in your town who are similarly minded. You may want to consider organizing your own *Perfect Love* book discussion group. The "Perfect Love Reader's Guide" found on the Website can help you do just that.

Perhaps, in time, you'll discover that you enjoy each other's company so much you'd like to form a local chapter of the Perfect Love Network. You might consider inviting us to your town so we can spread the Love together! (See the Website for details.)

Stop in at www.soulsailing.com today and see what all the excitement is about. We're eager to meet you there!

Heart to Heart Press

is dedicated to producing books and resources that support people on their journeys to Spirit-filled living.

We are committed to joining with others to create a global community rooted in compassion, peace, and prosperity for all.

For a complete list of books, products, and programs, visit our Website, www.hearttoheartpress.com.

Heart to Heart Press
P. O. Box 427,
Traverse City, MI 49685

(800) 831-3230

email: info@hearttoheartpress.com